Half-Jew

Searching for Identity

By D.M. Miller

Other books by D.M. Miller:

The Religion of the Heart
Agony of the Heart
Secrets of the Heart
Dandelion Fuzz

Half-Jew: Searching for Identity

D.M. Miller

ISBN-13: 978-1542348904

ISBN-10: 1542348900

Cover design by: kihani-design.com

For Esther

Contents

Preface

No one appointed me "Ambassador of the Half-Jews to the Rest of the World." To suggest there could possibly be a single voice for all is too one-dimensional for my taste, and as the saying goes, life is not black and white but shades of grey. We Half-Jews happen to be within that color spectrum, closer to one end or the other or somewhere in between. As a writer, all I can do is convey my own story and present my arguments. Everyone has the right to agree or disagree, and I have no doubt there will be lots of both.

The intention here is not to offend anyone, though challenging long-observed ideas is bound to generate an emotional response, either positive or negative but passionate to some degree. It is also important to note, I am neither promoting nor discouraging interfaith relationships but rather, shedding light on what it is like to be the product of such a marriage, along with the struggles I have faced on a personal level in terms of this topic.

We all have to find our place in this world, and like it or not, people fall into groups, categorized like products being sorted at a factory, labeled and pushed in one direction or another. But what if there is no perfect fit? What if you don't meet the requirements for this or that, or you are disqualified on a technicality? Is there an answer? Is there a solution?

What I ask is for those rigid in their beliefs to read with an open mind before disregarding the book right from the get-go with the standard reaction ingrained since childhood that there is no such thing as a "Half-Jew" because... It's like flipping a switch. The term "Half-Jew" is met with intense resistance, a swift kick to the gut and a big, fat "No!" That angry response is not consistent with those who are otherwise compassionate and caring, and there is no need to alienate this growing demographic. Just take a deep breath, read my arguments, my words, my story, and understand my perspective.

Introduction

I am a Jew. How I've longed to say those words without the long, drawn-out explanation. Am I lying when I say it? Do I have a right to make this claim? And why are the answers to these questions complicated enough for me to dedicate an entire book to exploring the issue?

Well maybe because, quite frankly, it *is* complicated.

Jews are a unique people unlike any other, a people whose nearly 6000-year history is filled with both light and darkness, love and hate, and good and evil. They are a people who have escaped total annihilation through a series of pogroms scattered across the world, inquisitions and ethnic cleansings, (the worst of course being the Holocaust, or Shoah, and Hitler's Final Solution), but they are also the people of the Bible, the Torah and Tanakh.

Jews are descended from Abraham, Isaac and Jacob. When God told Abraham, He would make of him a great nation,[1] that great nation became the Jewish people.

Unfortunately, it hasn't been an easy ride. Jews are both blessed and plagued with a rich yet troublesome history. They are God's chosen people but also the target of a constant and exaggerated, rabid hatred from their fellow man. As such, it is imperative to define just who exactly is a Jew and why. Well, there is an answer according to Jewish scholars, but it has become far less straightforward than it should be. Oh sure, the basic answer is that if your mother is a Jew, you're a Jew. Period. But as a Half-Jew, it will never be as simple as that for me. Nor am I alone.

Jews in Diaspora have intermarried to a great extent, a controversial issue in the religious community for a multitude of reasons. But here's the thing: people fall in love. The Jews who live outside of Israel have a greater possibility of falling in love with a non-Jew because we live and work with and around many people. Not all of those people are Jews. What's more, a large percentage are not. After all, Jews only make up roughly 0.2 percent of the world population[2] with approximately 83 percent[3] of that 0.2 living in either Israel or the United States.

The 83 percent is further broken down to about 43 percent in Israel and around 40 percent in the U.S. While that may sound like a lot, it amounts to a mere 5.7 million out of over 300 million, the total population of the United States.

Lots of numbers, but what it comes down to is the fact that only 2 percent or less of America's population is Jewish, and over 1 million are concentrated in New York City. According to one study, around 13 percent of America's Jewish population is in the "Big Apple" with another 7 percent in the city's suburbs.[4] More than 40 percent of America's Jews live in six states, but even in those six states, the populations are small by comparison.[5] This makes it a difficult task, a burden even, for many Jews, especially those who do not live in New York or those other five states, to find that perfect soul mate, one who also happens to be Jewish.

Yes, there is the local Jewish community, in many cases either small or nonexistent, and what are the chances of finding that special someone when the choices are so limited? It is more likely to meet and fall in love with someone from work, school or the neighborhood. And dating sites? Sure, Jewish dating sites exist today, but I've heard many complaints that people are still struggling to meet the right person. And besides, internet dating sites may help nowadays, but what about all the people married long before the world wide web came to be?

The reality is, we cannot dictate our emotions, and we simply fall in love with whomever we fall in love. The old-fashioned arranged marriage may still exist, but it certainly is no longer prevalent or ideal by modern standards. And while marrying within our religion makes sense, especially in terms of raising children, it is not always possible. For these reasons and more, many Jews in Diaspora marry non-Jews.

My father happened to be one of them.

A Jew in Diaspora

Most of my father's family lived in or around the Philadelphia area. His own parents had resided in the city but eventually moved to New Jersey, which is where my father grew up. Now there is a sizeable Jewish community in Philadelphia, but in the Pine Barrens region of southern New Jersey, which is basically considered the boondocks, there are few Jews, far fewer still back when my father was a young thing.

Living Away from the Jewish Community

The part of New Jersey where my dad, and later I, were raised, was about as rural as it gets. It was common to pass horse and dairy farms, cornfields and other crops while driving down the road, and many families had vegetable gardens or at least patches of flower beds spread around their yards. Farm stands were scattered across the area where the locals could get the best sweet, white corn around, Jersey tomatoes, or other produce native to the area. To this day, my favorite apple cider of all time was produced at a local orchard where payment was received at an unmanned store, based on the honor system. There are even a few permanent farm stands, seasonal of course, that are quite large because there is so much grown in South Jersey. People from New York who only go so far into New Jersey to dip their toes in, seem to think the state is all about the smelly oil refineries up north, the Atlantic City casinos and the Jersey shore, but in reality, New Jersey has earned its moniker "The Garden State" for all the wonderful farming down south. Unfortunately, many of those farms have since become housing developments, but that's another story.

Where there aren't crops or animals there are trees, loads of them. The Pine Barrens has become a protected region, and residents need to get government permission to cut down trees, or else the charm of the place would disappear in a sea of rooftops, many of which are getting bigger and bigger. South Jersey has attracted plenty of wealthy city folk from Philadelphia and New York who have come and built their mansions. But during my childhood and even more so during my father's, the Pine Barrens was woodsy, thick with pine, oak, maple, birch and other trees, brush, bushes, flowers, etc., and you'd have to take a close look to find a house here and there behind it all. There are also churches dotting the landscape, especially in the quaint little towns, some of which, established as early as the 1600s. My own hometown has houses dating back to the late 1700s.

Beautiful, right? But synagogues? Not a single one around, at least that was the case years ago. There are Catholic and Protestant churches and Quaker Friends meeting houses, but no synagogues. The reason for that is quite simple: no Jews. Except for my family, that is.

Anti-Semitism in a Small Town

Now the locals didn't take too kindly to Jews invading their turf, and if family folklore is true, my grandfather wanted to buy a house in an affluent and somewhat exclusive neighborhood in New Jersey but was denied because Jews were not allowed. My grandfather was quite a character from what I'm told—(he died before I was born, so I don't have firsthand knowledge)—and he would not let some snobby, well-to-do, arrogant anti-Semites get away with that. He hired an attorney and took the case all the way to the New Jersey Supreme Court—and won!

While that's all well and good, it did not erase the anti-Semitism of the time or the region, and my father was one of the only Jews in his high school, where classmates called him "(the N-word) Hair" for what is now affectionately known as a "Jew-fro." Many Jews do not have curly hair, but there

13

are those of us who do have the stereotypical Jewish 'fro, and my father was one of them.

Yes, Jewish hair really is "a thing." I've seen articles about it, notably one written by Leah Berkenwald entitled, "What Is Jewish Hair?",[6] in which the author describes the dark, curly, frizzy hair that is a sort of signature of some Jews. It also apparently is a target for anti-Semitism as my father experienced growing up in this rural Jersey town.

This is merely a snapshot of the anti-Semitism my father and his parents experienced back then, but enough, I hope, to paint a picture.

Under the circumstances, although my father was deeply proud of being a Jew with an inherent love for Israel, he was not particularly religious and clearly wanted to fit in with the people around him. With the last name of Miller, a surname which could be German or Irish (though because of name changes, it has also become the third most common Jewish surname in the United States,[7] a fact few realize), and with a paler skin tone, (rather than olive), and hazel eyes (even a red mustache when he grew one), my father's physical "Jewishness" slipped under the radar for the most part after he graduated from high school where everyone knew he was a Jew. And he apparently liked it that way, though it did invite so-called friends to openly divulge their hatred for Jews right to his face, not knowing with whom they were speaking or that underneath his shirt was a Star of David on a chain which he wore every day of his life.

This phenomenon was much like the old Paul Newman movie, *Exodus*, which contains a scene where a British officer goes on and on about how much he hates Jews and can spot one a mile away, while Newman, playing the part of the Jewish Ari Ben Canaan, asks him to check and see if there's something in his eye. The man looks directly in his eye without realizing he is standing there with one of those Jews he hates so much. (Incidentally, Newman himself was a Half-Jew.)

Believe it or not, my father, as strong of a personality as he had and as opinionated, aggressive and hot-tempered as he was, would often say nothing, rarely admitting he was a Jew, except to Jewish friends. Time and time again, I would overhear his friends with their anti-Semitic comments, and my blood would boil.

I clearly remember one time storming out of the room, and my father followed me. He told me that it angered him as well but that I should calm down. I really don't know why he didn't tell them to shove it "where the sun don't shine," but he didn't, perhaps taking enjoyment in the fact that he could pass as a Gentile and hear how they felt about Jews when they talked to each other.

The point is, living in Diaspora and in a non-Jewish community, while proud of being a Jew, my father also wanted to fit in. More than anything, he did not want to be restricted to marrying a girl chosen by his parents. And they sure tried. His mother set him up on date after date with Jewish girls she found (who knows how), but he never did click with any of them and couldn't find the right girl.

The Right Girl

And then one day, he did. He was 22 years-old and driving down the road when my mother passed. Being a naïve and friendly girl, she waved to him. The thing is, she knew who he was. Not only did they attend the same high school all four years and elementary school in eighth grade, but my father was also dating my mother's neighbor at the time.

Somehow my father didn't know who my mother was and thought she was waving to flirt—or so he said. There was a corner store she visited every day to get the mail and pick up a few items for her mother, and after the wave, my father pulled in and started his own flirting.

15

Another day, he saw her at the store again, not realizing she went there every day and claiming, playfully, that she was following him. Though reluctant at first because of her neighbor, my mother eventually decided to date my father. She was enamored after all, because despite the anti-Semitism in high school, my dad was somewhat of a star as a musician whose main instrument was the accordion. Back then, the accordion was more popular than it is now, and my mom had heard him playing beautifully during school assemblies. She also was aware he could play various other instruments and was blown away by his talent. It may sound strange now, but it was akin to girls going gaga over singers or actors today.

An interfaith relationship ensued. He was a Jew. She was a Catholic—and not just any Catholic—a German.

Who Is a Jew?

The Religious Arguments

Renowned rabbi and author Lord Jonathan Sacks has a touching video called, "Why I Am a Jew,"[8] where he provides a wonderful explanation of what makes him a Jew. It's about Judaism itself, morality, God, Torah and its teachings, among other things. But he also mentions being a child of his people, the hopes and dreams of his ancestors living on in him and inheriting all that Judaism is from his parents and their parents before them. As I understand it, he is not referring to his ancestral ties in terms of DNA but to something far deeper. I, however, will discuss both because there is an interconnectedness that exists between the two.

It may be a controversial concept, but the fact is, Jews are an ethnoreligious group. What does that mean? Quite simply, both an ethnicity and a religion rolled into one. Get it? Don't worry if you don't. It is an idea so difficult to grasp, most people, both Jewish and non-Jewish alike, deny, ignore, or misunderstand, causing such confusion, the basic concept becomes a mess for all except one—the Half-Jew. The Half-Jew knows exactly what it means.

But there is no such thing as a Half-Jew! That's what they claim. Either you're a Jew, or you're not, but I can assure you, when your father is Jewish but your mother is not, you will cling to the Half-Jew label because it is better than nothing at all.

Later in the book I will explain the "ethno" part of ethnoreligious, but in this chapter, I will focus on the religious explanation of who is a Jew and who is not.

According to Halakhah, which is Jewish or rabbinic law, the definition of a Jew is quite simple: If your mother's a Jew, you're a Jew, no matter who your father is. If your mother is not a Jew, you're not a Jew, again, no matter who your father is.

While the rule may be straightforward, the reasons why are not as easy to accept, especially when considering the fact that Atheists with a Jewish mother are still Jews, and secular Jews who have never seen the inside of a synagogue and know nothing of Jewish traditions or history are also Jews if they have a Jewish mother (that is, one who was Jewish when they were born—if the mother converted to Judaism after the birth of a child, that child is not Jewish).

An example: I once had a friend whose mother was Jewish and his father, Christian. My friend attended a private Christian school all throughout elementary and high school. He didn't know which religion was right but never went to synagogue and knew little about it. Then when he got married, he happened to marry a Jew—in the synagogue—with no need to convert because after all, he was already a Jew. Mother's a Jew, you're a Jew.

Another friend of mine with a Jewish mother and Christian father grew up in the Soviet Union. His mother taught him nothing about Judaism, but he did know a bit about Christianity. He knew no Jewish traditions, nothing about the holidays, no Hebrew, nada. All he knew was that he loved Israel because his mother instilled it in him.

When the Soviet Union fell, he, along with many other Soviet Jews, Half-Jews and even Quarter-Jews, left for Israel. He became Israeli and was a Jew, without a doubt. Mother's a Jew, you're a Jew.

I have on occasion asked him religious questions, to which he has laughed and told me I was asking the wrong person, that I know far more about Judaism than he. Then I thought he would at least know about holiday traditions, and even living in Israel, he still could not answer me. I suppose it's because he married a Christian, so he never had personal experience with observing a Jewish holiday, despite living in the Jewish State.

My friend and I are both Half-Jews. However, he is the "right" half, while I am the "wrong" half, thereby making him a full Jew and me, a Gentile.

Another Half-Jew named Shmuel[9] is the right half: His mother is Jewish, making him Jewish by default. Still, he was raised in an interfaith household, and I asked him to tell me a little about it.

"My father was not Jewish. Mom and maternal side, Polish Jewry. We kinda straddled the 'fence' when growing up. Dad's side, Finnish/Catholic. It wasn't until I joined the military when I decided to embrace my Jewish side fully, and it's been a wonderful journey ever since."

So how was he raised religiously speaking?

"We were pretty much Passover/Yom Kippur Jews and Easter/Christmas Catholics."

An interfaith upbringing, but it was easy for him, with a Jewish mother, to slide into Judaism without converting. I asked Shmuel why he went in that direction, whether the military acted as a catalyst somehow or if it was simple maturity.

"Well, I do not believe it was the military specifically, but a yearning I had for quite some time. Personally, I was always drawn more to my Jewish side. The military made me think of my own mortality, and embracing Judaism seemed more real," he explained.

Great story, and I'm happy for Shmuel, but it's more difficult for a Half-Jew with a non-Jewish mother.

Now if someone with a Jewish father but non-Jewish mother is raised in the Jewish tradition, observing Shabbat (the Sabbath) and the holidays, eating kosher, attending synagogue, fasting for Yom Kippur, the whole bit, is not a Jew without converting, but an Atheist with a Jewish mother is 100 percent Jewish, something is amiss.

Fortunately, there are Reform rabbis who will accept paternal lineage if the person in question was raised with Judaism. However, the Orthodox and other denominations don't care what Reform rabbis have to say about it and will never accept paternal lineage no matter what anyone proclaims. So if you grow up in a Reform synagogue, and you think you're a Jew because of your paternal lineage, think again. The Orthodox will tell you to convert if you want to call yourself a Jew. That goes for converts who converted in a Reform synagogue as well. It doesn't count in Orthodox Judaism, so be prepared for the ol' "you're not a Jew" lecture. Spent a lot of money on your conversion? Too bad!

The Easy Answer

As for the reasons why, I have heard various answers. It all depends on who is explaining. There are some who will simply say it is because there will never be any doubt as to who your mother is, but the father's identity could be questionable. This is the reason Rabbi Alfred J. Kolatch explains in his book, *The Jewish Book of Why.*[10] He also writes that if the Jewish mother later converts to another religion, it will not affect the child's natural right to be Jewish.[11]

That means that if the mother is Jewish at the time of her child's birth but converts to Catholicism a week later, never teaching her son or daughter a thing about Judaism, that child is still a Jew.

If this is the true reason for the rule in this day and age when paternity is easily checked through DNA testing, has this argument not become obsolete?

Other rabbis, however, provide different explanations. But before examining them, let's first keep in mind that while one's Jewishness is determined by maternal lineage, tribal affiliation was always passed down through the father. Make sense? No?

The Torah is very much about the men, isn't it? While there is also a lot written about the women, all the "begots" are told through paternal lineage. Genesis 5 begins the lineage from Adam, telling of how Adam had Seth and other sons and daughters. Then Seth begot Enosh and more sons and daughters. Enosh begot Kenan, Kenan begot Mahalalel, etc., all the way to Noah, who begot Shem, Ham and Japheth. [12]

There were other sons and daughters, but we are told only of the important ones, all men. Who were the wives of these men? Who were the mothers of the sons who were important enough to mention? They are not named here. The lineage is told strictly through the men.

In Genesis 11, there was more "begotting" going on. We are told the lineage of Shem, only the important sons, all the way down to Abram and Lot. Men, men, men. Then in Genesis 35, we get to the very important 12 sons of Jacob, important because from them we get the 12 tribes of Israel. In this case, we are told who the mothers are, but remember, the head of each tribe was a son of Jacob, not a daughter.

The following chapter details Esau's descendents, the clan of this and the clan of that, all from Esau's sons, not daughters.

On the other hand, God gave land to Abraham's line through Isaac, [13] his son with Sarah, rather than through Ishmael, his son through Hagar. Though God said he would make a great nation out of Ishmael, [14] (and the result is 22 Arab nations today), God told Abraham that His covenant would be everlasting with Isaac and his descendants. [15] While this was before actual "Judaism," if Sarah is the mother of all Jews, [16] was this done because Sarah was the "Jewish mother," while Hagar was not?

According to Jewish writer Mordechai Housman, [17] technically Sarah and Abraham were converts, and the covenant was with Isaac rather than Ishmael, not because of who Hagar was but because Ishmael did not choose to serve God while Isaac did.[18] Therefore Ishmael, with a Jewish father and non-Jewish mother, was not a Jew but became the father of the Arabs, and it had to do more with choices rather than ancestry.

Really?

But then Housman goes on to make the point that both Jacob and Esau had the same mother and father, yet Jacob was Jewish and Esau was not because Jacob chose to serve God.

Okay, but it's important to note that the Torah does not state that matrilineal ancestry determines one's Jewishness. Nowhere does it say such a thing, and with all the laws laid out in the Torah, 613 to be exact,[19] which include laws on marriage and sexual conduct, where is the explicit rule dictating that, well, if your mother's a Jew, you're a Jew?

It isn't there because it doesn't exist.

But all right. Let's review the arguments.

Deuteronomy 7:1-5

Rabbis and others who explain this issue often refer to the same few verses as evidence. First up is Deuteronomy 7. As the chapter begins, it is rather obviously written about entering the Promised Land, not a general instruction for all eternity. It states that when God delivers the Jews to this Holy Land, there will be seven nations to be defeated: the Hittites, Girgashites, Amorites, Canaanites, Perizzites, Hivites and Jebusites.[20] God commands the Jews not to intermarry with them[21]—"them," as in, the people of these specific nations, the Hittites, Girgashites, etc.

I have heard it argued that in Hebrew, the language is worded in a way that makes it a commandment forevermore, and who am I to argue with learned rabbis who spend their lives poring over the Torah? However, from my very simple-minded perspective, (along with common sense), I see these seven nations listed, the order to destroy them and the command not to intermarry with them but to completely defeat them, making no covenant with them and showing them no favor.

Now if these verses were an eternal commandment for how Jews are to interact with Gentiles, wouldn't it apply, not only to intermarrying but also to not showing them any favor and to not making any covenant with them? And yet, Jews do of course come to agreements with non-Jewish nations all the time. If not, there would never be any peace, however, Jews are constantly extending the olive branch. Simply put, how can the order to destroy the seven nations be specific to that instance, while the intermarrying prohibition is nonspecific, applying to any Gentile anywhere, anytime?

The following verse is the controversial one. It states that the reason why the Jews should not intermarry with these people is because they will cause them to turn away from God.[22] But what is the correct translation from the Hebrew? In the JPS translation,[23] it uses the non-gender specific word "children" when it says that intermarrying will cause them to turn against God.

However, the version used by Chabad online,[24] is translated with the word "son" when stating that intermarrying will cause the men to turn away from God, thereby providing evidence that if the Jewish men intermarry with non-Jewish women, the men will turn away from God.

It certainly seems petty to be analyzing this thing to death, but it makes me wonder which translation is correct or if it even matters. First, it says that neither the Jewish men nor women should intermarry. Then, if the translation is correct, it says that they shouldn't intermarry because the men will turn away from God. Yet immediately before this command prohibiting intermarriage, it is very clearly specific to entering the Promised Land and defeating those seven nations. And immediately following the intermarriage verse, God tells them that instead of intermarrying with them, they should tear down and burn their altars and other things dedicated to worshipping other gods.[25] Is that not specific again to defeating these particular seven nations?

Therefore, do we have a verse specific to a place and time, followed by a general verse, which is then followed by another verse specific to that place and time? Or are all three verses actually targeting that particular instance and those particular people?

The Book of Ezra

The next argument comes from Chapters 9 and 10 of the Book of Ezra. It is yet another story, specific to a certain place and time and hinging on particular circumstances. On the other hand, Bible stories teach us lessons to carry with us throughout our lives and over the course of time, though it is important to remember, the interpretation of whatever lesson we should be learning is open to debate.

As the Book of Ezra begins, we learn that the reign of King Cyrus of Persia has just begun. Prompted by God, the king called on the Jews to rebuild the temple in Jerusalem in Judah. Many of the exiles returned from Babylon to the holy city.

In Ezra 2, there is a list of all who returned, explained, as usual, in terms of "the sons of" this man and that man. (Their mothers were not named, as their lineage was told through their fathers' names.) Altogether, it amounted to over 42,000 people not including their servants.

In Chapter 3, the Israelites are now back, each in his respective hometown, and they all come together with a common goal: to worship God and rebuild His house.

Later they run into some problems, but the building again resumes under King Darius, thought by some to be the son of Queen Esther,[26] which would make him (according to "the mother law") a Jew himself, though there is no mention of such a thing. To be fair, it is also argued this was a different Darius, as experts can't seem to agree.

Incidentally, Queen Esther was a Jew who married a Persian, an interfaith marriage encouraged by Esther's cousin and foster or adopted father[27] Mordechai. Though the Persian king was not aware he was marrying a Jew until long after the fact, he was in love with her and that love, that marriage, that interfaith alliance, was what ultimately saved the Jews from annihilation in the Book of Esther, now celebrated during the holiday of Purim. It's quite something really that this interfaith union, which was pushed by Esther's adopted father Mordechai, now eternally revered by the Jewish people for his role in saving the Jews from a complete genocide, is never used as an argument against the supposedly "general" instruction by God in Deuteronomy 7 not to intermarry.

And if it was Esther's son who played a role in getting the second temple rebuilt, this interfaith relationship served yet another purpose to the benefit of the Jewish people. As I already stated, however, we do not know whether or not this is truly the case.

In any event, the temple was finished on the third of the month of Adar during Darius' sixth year as king[28] (around 350 B.C.E.). The Book of Ezra is far from vague in giving us the exact time of completion. Nothing general about it.

Then, in Chapter 9 of Ezra, something happens. We are told that the Jews have not separated themselves from the non-Jews there, and those non-Jews keep the same "abhorrent" practices like those of the Canaanites, Hittites, Perizzites, Jebusites, Ammonites, Moabites, Egyptians and Amorites.[29] Notice some of the same peoples are listed in the Deuteronomy verses we've already examined.

Not only did the Jews neglect to separate themselves from these other people, but they also married their women and the "holy seed" mixed with them, these foreign women.[30]

The remainder of Chapter 9 describes Ezra and his anguish over this terrible transgression. He tears his clothes, pulls out hair from both his head and beard, and cries over the humiliation as he prays and prays.

In Chapter 10, it is decided that in order to reconcile with God, the guilty men who intermarried with the foreign women must send them away.[31] This includes the children they had had with them. It is a long process, and to bring even more shame upon the guilty parties, these men who intermarried are named—the men, that is, and their male offspring who also intermarried. The names of the men are listed as "the sons of" their fathers, not their mothers. Not one mother's name is listed. (These women are not worth naming, despite their invaluable role of passing down one's Jewishness.)

Everyone was regretful and repented by sending away their foreign wives and children.

It certainly makes a strong case against intermarrying, and the example here is Jewish men marrying foreign women. But should it be taken within the context of this particular place and time, or should it apply to Jewish men forevermore?

We are told these people had abhorrent practices. Does that mean that all non-Jews have abhorrent practices because they do not follow Jewish law? Or was this meant to be about these particularly awful people?

Worshipping idols, for example, is a big no-no in the Torah. Worshipping other gods. But Christians, for example, worship the same God. As such, would the Christians of today be thrown into the same pot of horrid people as the Canaanites, Hittites, Amorites, etc.? And as time moves on, people change and the circumstances and places change, is it still possible to look at Scripture so detailed and so specific and apply it unequivocally to every situation in every place and at any time until the end of the world? Or should it be amended with modern rulings or at least revisited on a case-by-case basis?

Certainly if everyone intermarried, it could be the end of the Jewish people if the spouses did not convert to Judaism. Of course this is a complaint that some have regarding Jews in Diaspora, losing their Jewishness and not having Jewish offspring. In my case, however, the Jewish line could have continued had I been accepted as a Jew. Unfortunately, the "wrong" parent was the Jew, and that is the issue at hand.

Do the religious arguments make sense? And what about the ethnic side of things?

The Ethnic Jew

Many people refuse to accept the fact that Jews are indeed an ethnoreligious group. We have Hitler to thank for that. Had Hitler not focused on "Jewish blood," there would be far less confusion today regarding the ethnicities of Jews, but because of his hatred and evil acts, the public narrative changed. "Jewish blood? What Jewish blood? There's no such thing! It's a religion, not an ethnicity!"

Wrong. It's both. And this is not something I'm making up. There have been so many genetic and DNA studies done on Jews, it would be absurd to pretend there is no "Jewish people."

Jewish Converts

But what about the converts? They are every bit as Jewish as those with Jewish heritage. That is absolutely correct, however, there are few converts because unlike Christianity or Islam, there is no proselytizing in Judaism. No evangelism. Jews do not go out purposely seeking new adherents, and the tiny number of Jews existing in the world today, 0.2 percent of the entire world population, proves that fact. Therefore, the limited number of converts is not enough to disregard the majority of Jews who do have ethnic Jewish heritage.

When Your Father Doesn't Count

Does it matter? It does when you are ethnically Jewish on your father's side, but people want to erase your father's ethnicity completely from your heritage, making claims which essentially amount to saying that you are only what your mother is, and your other half counts for nothing at all. Zero. Zilch. Your father's side is merely a void, a vacuum, and it doesn't matter if you look like him, act like him or feel an inexplicable pull to Israel and to the Jewish people. A love. A longing. Something which cannot be taken away from you, whether others accept it or not.

Take the example of a man who is, let's say, Irish on his mother's side and Japanese on his father's side. He's a mixture of both parents, as we inherit half our genes from our mother and half from our father, but in this case, his father's traits are more evident. He looks like his father, and everyone says it. But then, let's pretend the rule is, he is not Japanese. He can only be what his mother is because his father doesn't count.

Really? Does that sound logical?

We can examine example after example using various races, which can clearly demonstrate on a physical level the absurdity of discounting the father's genes. A white mother and black father. The child has attributes from both parents, but it is impossible to deny certain physical traits from the father.

An English mother and Italian father. A Russian mother and Pacific Islander father. A Peruvian mother and Nigerian father. A Spanish mother and Chinese father. A Norwegian mother and Tunisian father. The potential combinations are practically limitless, and in each example, it would be impossible to deny the father's heritage, especially if it is clearly visible from a physical standpoint. It's simple common sense.

However, when your heritage inherited from your father is Jewish, suddenly, it does not exist. You're not a Jew, and it doesn't matter if you look just like your father and nothing like your mother. You're what your mother is, and that's all.

Sure. Now let's get real.

Jewish Ethnicities

Jews do have an ethnicity,[32] and their ethnicity is mostly distinct from that of the people of their host nations.[33] In other words, a Russian Jew is not Russian like an ethnic Russian. A British Jew is not ethnically English, Irish, Scottish or Welsh. A Spanish Jew is not ethnically Spanish, and a Moroccan Jew is not ethnically Moroccan. These Jews are ethnically Ashkenazi, Mizrahi or Sephardi, all terms which many people have never heard of in their lives. And that is why it is easier to simply say that they are Jews. Period.

What do those three ethnicities mean anyway? What are they?

These three ethnicities are practically the same. The Ashkenazim (plural for Ashkenazi) are European Jews;[34] the Mizrahim are Middle Eastern Jews; and the Sephardim are Spanish Jews.[35] Often times the Sephardim and Mizrahim[36] are grouped together because many of the Spanish Jews returned to the Middle East after the Spanish Inquisition. Also in the Middle East today, most Jews are in Israel since they were almost completely ethnically cleansed from Arab Middle Eastern countries, but in Israel, there is a mixture of Jews from all over the world, who have been intermarrying, Ashkenazim with Mizrahim, etc.

Even without intermarriage, studies have found the people who make up these three Jewish ethnicities are closely related to each other, more so in fact, than to the people of their host nations. So a Jew is a Jew whether he lives in Russia, Britain, America, Morocco, or Israel. Ethnically speaking, a Jew is a Jew, and religiously speaking as well.

How can this be? Because Jews are a people of course. Jews originated in the Middle East. Read the Bible. It's all in there. Jews can trace their lineage all the way back to Adam and Eve, if you take those early stories literally, and if not, at least from Abraham. There may be some gaps in knowing the full family lineage where the Tanakh left off and modern history began, but it's safe to say that Jews know exactly where they came from, and Israel is their ancestral homeland.

Bear in mind, there are some other smaller Jewish groups, apart from the big three named above. DNA studies have demonstrated some differences between the other groups and the main three, possibly because of isolation during certain periods in history or in some cases due to conversions or intermarriage. These other Jewish groups include Ethiopian Jews (Beta Israel),[37] Indian Jews (Bene Israel), Chinese Jews (Kaifeng), and Tunisian Jews (Teimanim), among others.

There is a claim that Ethiopian Jews are from the lost tribe of Dan, and that claim is accepted by some but denied by others who believe Ethiopian Jews are ethnic Ethiopians who converted somewhere along the line. From a religious standpoint, it matters not. During Operations Moses, Joshua and Solomon,[38] Israel rescued thousands of Beta Jews from Ethiopia and Sudan, bringing them to the Holy Land to escape persecution in Africa. They are Jews, and it doesn't matter if they are ethnic Jews or not; they are Jewish religiously nonetheless.

Religious perspective aside, the question is, why deny the Jewish heritage of those who are ethnically Jewish from their paternal lineage? And if ethnicity matters not, why accept those who reject Judaism only because they are ethnically Jewish from their maternal lineage or simply because when they were born their mother was a Jew, at least religiously speaking?

What I'm searching for here is logic.

DNA and Genetic Studies

Human beings are said to be 99.9 percent identical in our genetic make-up. That figure is now being refuted, though scientists are still putting our similarities at somewhere between 99 and 99.9 percent.[39] [40]

While it may seem I'm on a quest to seek out our differences, that is not exactly the case. We are all human beings and share a plethora of common traits, which should lead us to peace and love, not to the hatred which is far too abundant in this world. With that said, we are also individuals, always on the lookout for what makes us unique, but at the same time, we tend to be somewhat tribal by nature. Sure, much of the modern world (the Western world at least) has let go of the traditional idea of formal tribes, however, we still gravitate toward groups with common interests. That may be in a social setting, where people form cliques, or it may be according to religion, culture, nationality, ethnicity, race, gender, socio-economic class or all of the above. We gravitate toward people with a common interest, whatever interest that may be.

Who Am I? Searching for Answers

It is perfectly normal to ask, who am I, where do I fit in, and where do I come from? Both religiously and ethnically, we want to know where we belong. As for me personally, half German and half Jewish, growing up, I never had a firm grasp of who I was religiously or ethnically.

Three out of my four grandparents had died before I was born, and the only living person from that generation was my mother's mother, i.e., my German grandmother. I absolutely adored her, but she was old, born at the turn of the century. She was already quite old when my mother was born, and so the whole time I knew her, she was hunched over and shrunken, with white hair and wrinkles galore. The worst part was that she was hard of hearing and senile, most likely suffering from an undiagnosed Alzheimer's or Dementia. Nevertheless, she was the only grandparent I had, and I loved her dearly, even if she couldn't hear me half the time.

Unfortunately, she was the only relative on my mother's side I really got to know well, and she died when I was 15. I had an aunt and two cousins who lived far away, whom I only saw once each year and briefly at that. The cousins were several years older than me. I also had another aunt close-by and got along well with her, but her husband was a rabid anti-Semite, anti-just-about-anyone actually (including "A-rabs" and "I-talians"—think Archie Bunker!), and he always made me grit my teeth. He and my aunt had four children, but again, they were four more cousins far too old to be my friends back then.

On my father's side, I knew absolutely no one. After his parents passed away, he isolated himself from his entire family, partly because he'd kept his interfaith marriage a secret, even from his own parents, and partly due to personal family issues.

So what did I know? There was no strong sense of family, apart from our nuclear family unit. And when it came to feeling a connection to my German side, there was nothing. As for my Jewish side, even my father was confused about the Jewish ethnicity. At that point, I'd never heard the word "Ashkenazi," or "European Jew," and I'm certain my father wasn't familiar with the term either. He seemed to be more confused than anyone, and he didn't exactly set things straight for me or my siblings.

We were told that my father was Jewish, but we were also told he was Russian. When people would ask my ethnicity (because it was more common back then for people to ask), I would say that I was half German and half Russian. (To which, my classmates in school would respond, "You're a Nazi and a Communist!" Right, a Jewish Nazi. My German family left Germany before World War II, and my Jewish family escaped Russia before the Bolshevik Revolution. But kids will be kids, and they didn't know any better. Still, it made me feel different, like I was an odd combination of ethnicities.)

Then sometimes I would say that I was half German and half Jewish, but I never really understood if I was Russian or Jewish or both.

Later on I started explaining that my father was a Russian Jew, but there was still that idea floating around that "Jew" referred to the religion of Judaism, and Russian was the actual ethnicity. That is incorrect, but no one explained it to me because they themselves didn't understand it.

Why? Again, because of Hitler. If it hadn't been for the Holocaust and the idea that if you had "Jewish blood," you could be sent to the ovens, I don't think people would ever have started to deny that Jews are indeed an ethnicity.

My father used to say he was Russian, but he would also tell me that one Jew always knows another. He would point out people and say that this one is a Jew and that one is a Jew. His theory made no sense. If he was Russian rather than ethnically Jewish, how would it be possible to tell by sight alone whether someone was Jewish? He wasn't indicating men wearing a kippah on their head, which would make it obvious. And of course, he was wrong anyway. It isn't always evident by looks alone whether someone is Jewish because Jews have various looks, and there are other Mediterranean people like Italians or Greeks who could be mistaken for being Jewish. And then there are Arabs, our cousins.

Many Jews admit that Arabs are our cousins, cousins that is, going back all the way to Abraham and his sons, Isaac and Ishmael. As the story goes, Jews descended from Isaac and Arabs from Ishmael, but both from Abraham, which is why we say that Judaism and Islam are Abrahamic religions. But if Jews are willing to admit that Arabs are our cousins, it follows suit that Jews are not just a religion but an ethnicity. Otherwise, how can Arabs be our cousins? And why do Arabs have an ethnicity, but Jews do not?

In fact, Arabs and Jews do share DNA, as studies have shown,[41] proving our common heritage yet again, in accordance with the Book of Genesis.

Even my father used to say that Jews and Arabs are the same ethnicity. He clearly spoke out of both sides of his mouth in saying we're the same ethnicity but then saying that he was Russian. Now which is it? Jewish or Russian? The answer is Jewish, but back then, I didn't understand, and many people still do not understand to this day.

Now with scientific studies, it is clear that Jews have a unique ethnicity, just as Italians do, or the Irish, the Chinese, the Indians or Arabs.

Whether people are willing to admit it or not, scientific studies have proven that Jews are a people, apart from a religion. It is not merely a case of a common culture, i.e., eating Jewish food, speaking Hebrew, Yiddish or Ladino, or wearing certain religious garb. Jews share a common lineage, which makes sense given that many of us are descended from Abraham, Isaac and Jacob, and the Jewish people have not intermarried as much as other groups of people. We are essentially, a family.

Crazy idea? Not at all.

Genetic Testing on Ashkenazi Jews

A study came out in 2014, revealing that all Ashkenazi Jews are cousins.[42] That's right. We are all a family. Descended from about 350 Middle Eastern and European Jews, Ashkenazim today are all at least 30th cousins. No wonder we feel a kinship; it is not merely a religious bond but is in our genetic make-up.

Not only that. Another study found that 40 percent of Ashkenazim descended from the same four women. The "signatures" of those four ladies are virtually absent from non-Jews and are hardly found in Jews who are not Ashkenazi.[43] This demonstrates a definite distinction between Ashkenazi Jews and other Jews, although we are still more closely tied to one another than to non-Jews.

While Ashkenazi Jews are said to have originated in central and Eastern Europe, Dr. Doron Behar of the Rambam Medical Center in Haifa, Israel, the lead author of the study, explained that ultimately, "they can be traced back to Jews who migrated from Israel to Italy in the first and second centuries."[44]

The doctor also stated that the four women inherited their genetic signatures from female ancestors in the Middle East but that in his study, he focused on the European descendants who came later because that is when the Ashkenazi population really took off.[45]

This reaffirms that Jews in Diaspora, including the Ashkenazim, came from Israel, our ancestral homeland, proven scientifically that what we know to be true in our hearts is indeed fact. It also allows medicine, science, history, archaeology and religion to work in concert with one another. (I mention archaeology because there have been several cases of Bible stories proven to be true through the diligent work of archaeologists.)[46]

Medical Genetics

Other studies have found particular diseases to be more prevalent among Ashkenazi Jews. Genetic testing of specific ethnicities has a medical basis in finding who may be more prone to this or that ailment. The field of medical genetics is meant to diagnose and manage hereditary disorders, and if you think about it, if a disease or disorder is passed down through the family or is more common among a certain group of people, we would be doing ourselves a disservice by being politically correct. Though we can pretend all we want that people are people, and there are no differences among us, genetic studies have proven there are differences which are important in order to map disease genes and figure out how to help those prone to certain diseases. Because of Hitler and his evil obsession with Jewish blood, we have denied the existence of Jewish blood or the Jewish "race," but political correctness has no place in medicine.

When people use the word blood in this context, it is common knowledge they are not using the word literally. Though the blood libel[47] [48] has been used to attack Jews throughout history and still exists today,[49] [50] [51] most prevalently in anti-Semitic societies, hopefully the general public is aware of the colloquial meaning of the word "blood" when it is used to refer to family or ethnicity. A blood relative, for example. And we Ashkenazim are blood relatives, the most distant of us all being 30th cousins, as we already know.

As for the Jewish "race", again, this has become more of a colloquial term. There really is no such thing as race.[52] There are ethnicities, but the word "race" is used in a general sense, usually in reference to skin color. When it comes to Jews, people use it in place of the word "ethnicity."

They should not offend anyone, but if the words "blood" and "race" are offensive because of the Holocaust and Nazi evil, (and I am absolutely sensitive to that as these horrors happened to my people), then let's change the words. It's semantics, really, but if it helps, we can call it whatever people want to call it, but it is what it is—a Jewish ethnicity or ethnicities. A Jewish people.

Imagine if there were an Italian religion. But there is also an Italian people. If someone has a German mother and Italian father and therefore doesn't count as an Italian religiously speaking (because the rules in this hypothetical situation are the same as the "mother rule" in Judaism), that person remains half Italian ethnically speaking. Whatever ailments affect ethnic Italians will also affect this "half-breed."

Another example would be Arabs. Not all Arabs are Muslim. Some are Christian, and some practice other religions, but the vast majority of Arabs are Muslim. The two are tightly tied together, so much so, that Islamic culture is intertwined with Arab culture. With that said, an Arab Atheist or Arab Christian is still Arab.

It is a difficult concept when it comes to Jews and Judaism because of the uniqueness that accompanies an ethnoreligious group. No example seems good enough to illustrate the point, but the point, nevertheless, must be made.

Medical genetics happen to be one field that proves the point. Pinpointing ethnicity matters, and it could even save your life.

According to The American Society of Human Genetics, approximately 3-7 percent of people will be diagnosed with some sort of genetic disorder "not including common disorders, such as cancer, diabetes, heart disease and psychiatric disorders."[53] Furthermore, "all diseases or medical conditions have a genetic component (except trauma)."[54] The study of DNA can help for early detection and treatment, and figuring out who is predisposed to certain diseases is important.[55]

Breast and Ovarian Cancer

Those who follow celebrity news may have heard of Angelina Jolie getting a double mastectomy because she tested positive for carrying a problematic BRCA1 gene, which indicates a greater risk for developing breast and ovarian cancer. After her mother's decade-long battle with cancer, the actress didn't want to take any chances, so she chose to be proactive.[56]

When Jolie made the announcement, she called attention to BRCA and the need to be tested, creating what became known as the "Angelina Jolie effect"[57]—the new trend of at-risk women getting tested for mutated BRCA1 or BRCA2 genes. Those considered high risk are people with a close relative who died prematurely from breast cancer but also people of Scandinavian descent as well as Ashkenazi Jews. It is believed that about 1 out of every 40 Ashkenazi women may have a mutated BRCA gene.[58]

The BRCA scare came about after a team of Israeli and American researchers published the results of a study which found that Ashkenazi women tested positive for mutated BRCA genes even with no family history of breast or ovarian cancer. Though not all carriers of the mutated genes will get cancer, a greater percentage of carriers get cancer than those who do not have the mutated gene.[59]

These findings have prompted doctors to recommend that all Ashkenazi women be screened as a precaution. The decision to move forward with a preventative double mastectomy and/or removal of ovaries and fallopian tubes has its risks as well, and is considered a controversial move by some.[60] Whatever decision the patient makes, at least we know the benefits of medical genetic testing.

More Jewish Genetic Diseases

Yes, there are differences among us genetically speaking.

According to the Jewish Genetic Disease Consortium (JGDC), anyone with at least one Jewish grandparent may be at greater risk than the general population for certain diseases, and they recommend screening for "Jewish genetic diseases," estimating that at least 1 in 3 American Ashkenazi Jews is "a carrier for at least 1 of 19 Jewish genetic diseases."[61]

The most well-known is Tay-Sachs Disease, with 1 in 27 Ashkenazi Jews afflicted.[62] The other 18 are: Bloom Syndrome, Canavan Disease, Cystic Fibrosis, Familial Dysautonomia, Familial Hyperinsulinism, Fanconi Anemia C, Gaucher Disease, Glycogen Storage Disease 1A, Joubert

Syndrome 2, Lipoamide Dehydrogenase Deficiency (E3), Maple Syrup Urine Disease 1B, Mucolipidosis IV, Nemaline Myopathy, Niemann-Pick Disease, Spinal Muscular Atrophy, Usher IF, Usher III, and Walker Warburg.[63]

The Jewish Genetic Disease Consortium recommends that all Jewish and interfaith couples be screened for Jewish genetic diseases, and this includes the Sephardim and Mizrahim.[64]

What's more, according to the Genetic Disease Foundation, the Mount Sinai Comprehensive Jewish Carrier Screening Panel covers 96 conditions relevant to one or all three of the major Jewish ethnicities of Ashkenazi, Sephardi and Mizrahi. There is also screening available for Beta-Thalassemia and Sickle Cell Anemia for African-Americans, and both Alpha-Thalassemia and Beta-Thalassemia for Asians.[65]

Jews are clearly not the only ones predisposed to certain disorders, and medical research has shown that race and ethnicity are factors in the development of specific diseases and disorders, as are the environment and culture. As a matter of fact, certain ethnic groups may be more likely to suffer particular ailments due to cultural habits or even socioeconomic variables,[66] but genetics can also play a role.[67]

Examining Our Differences

Concentrating on our differences is important when determining risk factors involved in the inheritance of genetic diseases, but there is nothing wrong with admitting we are different in a more general sense. When we are children, we are taught that we are all special, each one of us an individual. But as Western society has evolved, as adults, we are now taught that we are all the same, like some factory-made plastic containers, churned out side-by-side on the assembly line. We are meant to be color-blind, and if we see a bright pink container amongst the neutral beige, we are to ignore it, pretend we never saw it.

The problem is that the word "different" has somehow transformed its meaning to "value" or "worth." Different does not mean worth less or worth more. Equality is one thing, while uniqueness is another. Personally, I don't want to be a bland, plastic box. I want to be what I was taught as a child: an individual.

And as individuals, somewhat tribal by nature as I've already stated, we take pride in who we are and where we come from, which includes culture and heritage, even family history. But in growing up with a Jewish father and non-Jewish mother, I was made to feel my patrilineal side didn't count. Meanwhile, I had little connection to my matrilineage, apart from my mother and senile grandmother that is, as well as the occasional summer afternoons at my aunt's swimming pool and annual Christmas Eve visit to her house when she always had plates of various types of homemade Christmas cookies scattered around, with Bing Crosby serenading us in the background. These are warm memories, but this was the aunt who was married to the anti-Semite, which put a damper on the mood to put it mildly.

My father himself cut us off from his family, so in addition to being told I basically had no ethnicity on my father's side, I didn't know any of my Jewish relatives.

And yet—I loved them. And I loved the Jewish people as a whole. And I loved Israel. And I wept for my people who perished in the Holocaust—perished, at the hands of Germans... and I was German.

Anti-Semitism

While sitting in my living room one evening in August 2013, I was struck by what I saw on an episode of *Who Do You Think You Are?*, the television show sponsored by Ancestry.com, which films celebrities on their quest to follow a certain family line back through time. The episodes play out like a mystery, and each week, the guest celebrity visits genealogists, historians, museum curators and record keepers to get to the bottom of what happened to a particular family member. Sometimes it leads to the discovery of another mystery, and the story becomes tangible when the show brings the celebrity to the actual battlefield where the ancestor fought, or the house where the ancestor lived, and so on.

The episode which caught my attention[68] featured Chelsea Handler, a comedienne whom I sometimes watched on her late night talk show. Knowing virtually nothing about her until that time, I now learned that like myself, she was German on her mother's side and Jewish on her father's. She was raised Jewish, however, and considers herself a Jew, apparently having had a Bat Mitzvah in a Reform synagogue at the age of 12. (About a year after her episode of *Who Do You Think You Are?* aired, she posted a photo from her Bat Mitzvah on Instagram with the comment, "Don't ever say I'm not a real Jew."[69] Hmm... She must get the ol' "you're not a Jew if your mother's not Jewish" lectures too.)

As it turns out, she and I have many things in common oddly enough, but her story of having a German mother and Jewish father was what drew me into the show. You see, she worried about her grandfather's role in World War II.[70] Though identifying religiously with her Jewish side, she had German relatives who were also her family and also a part of who she was.

Nazis and Holocaust Victims: It's All in the Family?

I too have always wondered if any of my German relatives were Nazis. What an absolute horror that would be, to have some of my family gassed in the ovens and to have other family members pushing them in.

To be fair, I must admit that my maternal grandparents arrived in the United States as immigrants from Germany in the 1920s, and while my grandfather had served in the German army during World War I, he was already living in America during the Holocaust. As a matter of fact, my grandparents went back to Germany in 1939 with the intention of living there again, but my grandfather hated Hitler, badmouthing him every chance he could get, which frightened my grandmother. She ended up leaving, returning to America, and he followed later, having to escape at that point, slipping out through Holland.

And I must also admit that my paternal grandmother arrived in the United States as an immigrant around 1912/1913; my paternal grandfather was born in New Jersey, but his parents arrived in the United States around 1903.

This means that both sets of grandparents were already in America long before the Holocaust—no Nazis or Holocaust victims in my direct line. However, it's a safe bet there were both in my family tree—siblings of my grandparents, cousins, aunts, uncles, etc. It would be practically impossible for that not to be true; my Jewish family came from Eastern Europe, and my German family was in, well, Germany. There had to be both Nazis and Holocaust victims in the outer branches of my family tree.

And that is a tough pill to swallow.

The gut-wrenching reality of what my Jewish relatives went through, and the chilling possibility of unspeakable evil carried out by Germans who might also be distantly related to me. On both accounts, I'm sinking. Horrified and devastated. How? Just—how? And why?

Every Jew killed in the Holocaust was my cousin. We today are, after all, at least 30th cousins. And I grieve for them as my father grieved, reading the stories, watching movies, and making my mother feel guilty that her people did this to his people.

What an odd situation. My father defied his parents by marrying a non-Jew, and my mother defied hers by marrying a Jew. They ran off and eloped, marrying in secret because although my Jewish grandmother had met my mother and liked her, she wanted my father to marry a Jew. And my German grandparents were totally against my mother marrying a Jew. But then, though he had to marry her, my father would make my mother feel guilty about her German heritage.

As for me, growing up, I knew about the anti-Semitism on my German side. And it gnawed at me. How could they hate for no reason? And if they hated my father because he was a Jew, to me it meant they hated me too. I'm his offspring. I'm half him and half my mother. It wasn't true; they didn't hate me. But how could I feel any other way? If my father's a Jew, that makes me half Jewish, so if they hate Jews, they hate me.

And that is how I've always felt about anti-Semitism. Should I not take it personally? Should I not feel it because my mother's not a Jew? Forgive me, but that doesn't make one bit of sense. If people hate Italians, and your father is Italian, their Italian-bashing is going to affect you. If your mother is white, and your father is black, racist comments are going to tear you apart inside. After all, if your father's Italian, you're Italian. If your father's black, you're black. And if your father's Jewish, you're Jewish.

To feel that anguish and then be told, "Well, you're not actually Jewish because you're not a Jew if your mother's not a Jew," is just a slap in the face.

My father experienced enough anti-Semitism that he got to the point where he hid his Jewish identity, despite being proud enough to never remove the Star of David chain around his neck, (albeit buried under his shirt), despite his love for Israel, and despite his sorrow over his people murdered in the Holocaust. On one hand, he was a proud Jew, but on the other, he remained friends with anti-Semites and kept his mouth shut while they spewed their hatred right to his face. It was the strangest thing. He was an outspoken person, quick to temper and ready to unleash his anger at anyone who crossed him, but anti-Semitic friends were spared. Why? Because he wanted to fit in?

As far as I know, there was only one time that he finally said something, and it was a case of one comment too many. I guess he couldn't take it anymore with this particular friend, but did he scream and yell? Did he really let the guy have it? No. He simply said, "You know, not all Jews are like that."

Apparently it was enough to get the message. Afterwards, that friend and his wife would ask questions, "Do you people" do this or celebrate that? You people.

Anti-Semitism in My Own Life

Unlike my father, I didn't experience much anti-Semitism, apart from hearing his friends with their comments or my uncle by marriage. I did have a boss at one point when I lived down South (in the Southeastern part of the United States) who was telling me a story about negotiating for a new car, and she "Jewed the guy down." It was shocking how easily it flowed out of her mouth, but she quickly apologized, realizing her mistake at letting that one slip in front of me. I didn't take too kindly to it, and I reacted as a Jew, not as an outsider. Still, there was no direct discrimination, no consequences like the loss of a job or something worse.

There was another occasion in college at a bar, when a guy was trying to pick me up. I wouldn't have gone with him anyway, but for some reason I asked if he was Jewish. His response was jaw-dropping. A simple "no" would have sufficed, but instead I got an earful of how awful the Jews were and what an insult that I would dare suggest he could be one. He went on and on with his hatred, and when he was finished, he saw the horrified expression on my face, and the blood drained from his.

"You're Jewish, aren't you?" he asked me.

"Yup."

"And I just blew it, didn't I?"

"Yup."

Jerk.

The thing about anti-Semites is that they don't know who's a Jew and who isn't. They have no idea who it is they hate. Unless they see a kippah, sidelocks, a black suit and fedora, or unless they simply know because they know who the person is, they can never really be sure. Even the last name of Cohen doesn't necessarily mean the person is Jewish. After all, "if you're mother's not a Jew..."

If you're black, most people wouldn't dream of revealing their racism to you unless they're intentionally looking for a fight, but if you're Jewish and they don't know you're Jewish, you get to hear how they really feel. It's quite eye-opening how much hatred can be in one deranged mind. Even people who are seemingly nice can be filled with this unfounded hatred.

Some people are angry at the world, and they need a target. Jews have always been the world's punching bag, the scapegoat for everything that's wrong.

Gotta problem? Blame the Jews. Black plague? Jews' fault. Economic woes? Jews! Don't like your dictator? That's because he's influenced by the Jews, or—he has Jewish blood.

That's usually how the story goes anyway.

There are too many anti-Semitic canards to count: Jews killed Jesus; the blood libel which now includes organ harvesting; poisoning the wells; causing all the wars; exaggerating or fabricating the Holocaust; controlling the banks, the media, Hollywood and wanting to take over the world; etc., etc., etc. [71] [72] [73] [74] [75] [76] [77] [78] [79]

Jews are accused across the Middle East and Africa of spying with jinns as well as either spying or attacking with a whole menagerie of animals: birds more than anything, but also sharks, wild pigs, dolphins, and more. They are accused of stealing land, and have even been credited with ISIS. Yes, the Jews are behind ISIS, according to the same sort of conspiracy theorists who accuse Jews of being behind the 9/11 attacks. [80] [81] [82] [83] [84] [85] [86] [87] [88] [89]

I could go on and on about all the outlandish conspiracy theories against Jews, along with the attacks, murders and attempts at genocide over the course of history, the current threats and incitement to violence against Jews ever so present today, and I could list page after page of references for each topic. The point is, anti-Semitism is an old hatred, embedded in the minds of far too many people, and it has always affected me profoundly, whether I'm accepted as a Jew or not.

Back in 2011, when the Arab Spring was in full swing, I had a dream which inspired me to write my first novel in years, *The Religion of the Heart*. (The only novel I'd written before then was never published.) The dream itself was absolute nonsense but became the catalyst to get me writing again.

Since I knew there were many inaccuracies in this fantasy dream, after writing it all down in a period of only three weeks (yes, I was writing like a madwoman day and night), I set out to research, research, research, determined to make this novel not only enjoyable but correct in the religious and cultural details. Little did I know the journey upon which I was about to embark.

While most of my research was focused on legitimate and official sources, one less dependable route I decided to try was to venture into an online site. This well-known site has various categories, and Egypt happened to be one of them. Although this site was not meant to be a forum, that is exactly what it turned into.

Like everybody else, I chose a pseudonym for a screen name, and without considering the potential reactions to my alias, I picked a Jewish name which has special meaning to me.

That was, I suppose, a big mistake. Or perhaps, it was meant to be, to open my eyes. Why on earth I was oblivious to how real and widespread anti-Semitism is in the Middle East, is beyond me since I always knew it existed but somehow hoped that times had changed and people had been enlightened. How wrong I was.

The hippy dippy dream of those "coexist" bumper stickers and "can't we all just get along" is some kind of Western fantasy. It has absolutely no basis in reality, and it never will unless or until something changes in the leadership of nations which would rather blame the Jews for their own shortcomings. If they ever stop brainwashing the masses into believing that Jews are the root of all evil and accept the olive branch extended by Israel, we might actually get somewhere. But as long as anti-Semitic cartoons exist in their newspapers and in their television programming, as long as terrorists who murder Jews are celebrated as heroes and martyrs, as long as Holocaust denial and lies about Israel are taught in their schools, and as long as the UN and world media target Israel for simply being the Jewish State, anti-Semitism will flourish. 90 91 92 93 94 95 96 97 98 99 100

This was a hard lesson learned, but it started when I wandered into this forum on Egypt, largely visited by those claiming to be Egyptian and those searching for information like myself. I figured I would take what I found in there and later back it up with my own research to confirm or refute what they told me. That was really my goal.

Some of the respondents were helpful, others not so much. Though my questions at first were simple, unemotional and nonpolitical, many of the answers came in the form of attacks. But why, pray tell, were they jumping down my throat? It was the name, the Jewish name. I was informed I was a kike, unbeknownst to me, and other abusive language followed. How dare I, a Jew, (a kike I should say), invade their turf? And how interesting that when studying English, they're sure to learn the derogatory word for Jew.

There was no picture of me, mind you, no information about me whatsoever save the screen name I'd chosen. It was enough for the unleashing of hate to be thrown my way. And this was happening juxtaposed my own writing of an unparalleled love between an Egyptian man and Jewish woman. Guess a cold shower was warranted, and boy did I get one.

The experience was so nauseating, I needed a break from my research and decided to go into the category dedicated to Israel though it had nothing to do with my book. (Not that book at least—the sequel, *Agony of the Heart*, does mention Israel, and *Secrets of the Heart*, the third book in the series, has a chapter focused on Israel.)

I decided that I needed some comfort from my own people for a while. Little did I know, that forum was far more controversial than the one on Egypt, and some of the same anti-Semites from the other forum were even more active in the Israel category. That sent me on a mission to combat this anti-Semitism and anti-Zionism online and to do it with serious references and facts. Armed with truth, they had to listen, right?

Wrong. Only the fence-riders may listen, but the haters will hate no matter what. They do not listen to reason or hard facts. They hate Jews and hate Israel, and that is that.

Doing My Part to Combat the Hatred

Needless to say, my book got derailed for a while as I did what I could to defend my people against the growing online community intent on defaming Israel by making false accusations based purely on lying propaganda and spread so quickly it'll make your head spin. It's so easy to glance at headlines without reading the fine print and without checking the unreliable references used, if any are used at all. I had hoped at least some people would check these things and would actually read, which is why for some time, I continued to do what I could before realizing I had a far better vehicle at my disposal to get my point across: my novel.

There are many, many online warriors fighting for and against Israel and the Jewish people, but there are fewer novelists, using an entertaining fictional story to try to make a difference. Maybe I could clarify things a bit in a way in which people could relate, and maybe I could do it without some phony screen name but as myself. But this time, I don't have to feel guilty about "misleading" people into thinking I'm a Jew, whether I am or I'm not.

Some Jews tell me I am Jewish, or they tell me I have a Jewish neshama (soul), while others refuse to accept me as one of their own. As a novelist, it doesn't matter if I'm accepted as a Jew or not. I am simply writing and putting forth ideas, which I have found are relatable to Jews, Christians, secular Muslims and Atheists alike.

All I can do is write from my heart and let people love it or hate it. At least I know, Jewish or not, I can tell a story, which hopefully, in some small way, supports Jews, teaches readers facts they didn't know, and evokes some kind of an emotional response.

You see, whether I'm technically a Jew or not, the hatred against my people is one of the biggest themes of my life, and it dictates what I write. Violence against Jews and Israel is an injustice. I'm not a politician. All I know is writing, and if nothing else, I know I can point out this injustice in my own small way. As they say, the pen is mightier than the sword.

Interfaith Confusion

The confusing part about being a Half-Jew is that you're not fully in on either side. You're basically on the fringes of Jewish groups, who welcome your support and call you a friend but won't allow you to be dead smack in the middle of their circle. And if your other parent is Christian, you will never feel like you truly fit in with Christians either. There's something distinct about you, and you're just not "one of them," no matter how welcoming they may be. Deep down inside, you know you're different.

Neither, Nor

Much has been written about actor Jason Segel, who has spoken openly on having a Jewish father and Christian mother. Apparently, growing up, he attended a Christian school during the day and Hebrew school at night. On Marc Maron's *WTF* podcast,[101] Segel explained what that was like. "At Christian school you're the Jewish kid, and at Hebrew school you're the Christian kid. I think that's the nature of groups," he said. "And so everyone wants to compartmentalize people. And I think I decided at that point, like OK, it's me versus the world kind of."[102]

Maron, who is Jewish, threw that old familiar line at Segel. "Is your mom Jewish? No? You're not a real Jew."[103]

How many times have I heard that?

In high school, I read the Torah on my own and felt a deep connection to the Jewish faith and to the Jewish people. I knew I was a Jew. Though in grade school, there were no Jews as far as I knew, in high school, there were a few. I remember one year when every day I ate lunch with a group of girls, two of whom were Jewish. And there was an inexplicable bond, even though we never became close confidants.

But somehow, something was there, a "we're the same people" sort of tie. That's how I felt at least, but perhaps to them it wasn't the same as I was only half.

In health class one year, we had to pretend to be married to a classmate and take turns caring for an uncooked egg for a week as I recall, in order to simulate what it would be like to care for a baby. (Not many similarities there—no crying, no diapers to change, no getting up in the middle of the night or worrying over a sick child, but I suppose it was an introduction to the idea at least.) As a silly teenager, I told the only Jew in the class he had to be my husband for the experiment because we're both Jews. And he agreed! Whether or not he knew I was a Half-Jew is another story.

Then the summer after my junior year of high school, I attended Cornell University to take two six-week courses in a program designed for high school students. They were real Cornell courses however, and I received college credit for them, which later helped me get my B.A. one semester early.

The Cornell experience was the first time I'd left home for any extended period of time, and I stayed in a dormitory on campus. My roommate was Jewish, and we befriended two Jewish boys in the same program. Though we had other friends, the four of us became a tight group, spending most of our free time together. I was accepted by them but knew full well I was the only Half-Jew among them; they were the real Jews, and I was their half Jewish buddy. Still, it was the first time I felt like this was where I belonged.

After graduating from high school, I attended Syracuse University in upstate New York, where once again, my best friend was Jewish. We had a group of friends, the core of which comprised of all girls, mostly non-Jews, living on the same floor in the dormitory, but then we also knew other Jewish students. On Yom Kippur freshman year, my best friend and I got together with other Jewish friends to spend the day together, fasting, praying and discussing religion. Finally I felt like I fit in.

And then I was promptly told that I wasn't really one of them.

"You're a goy," a friend told me matter-of-factly.

The boldness of the remark stunned me. "How am I a goy?"

"If your mother's not Jewish, you're a goy."

The comment wasn't meant to be hurtful and was said in a lighthearted way, and yet, it tore me apart inside. Despite helping me in my spiritual journey and teaching me quite a bit about Judaism, my friend made it clear I didn't belong.

And how am I a goy when I feel Jewish, when ethnically, I'm half Jewish?

"If your mother's a Jew, you're a Jew. If your father's a Jew, you're nobody." Well, that's how it felt at least.

A Jew When You Want, A Goy When You Don't

What's interesting is the hypocrisy. On occasion, a Jewish magazine will have an article on "beautiful actresses you didn't know were Jewish," or something of that nature, and as you read it, you find that many are only Jewish on their father's side. Some may only be a quarter Jewish. But they're listed in the article because it's okay to accept Half-Jews as your own if you can take pride in claiming them. Beautiful actresses? Oh sure, they're Jews!

Nobel Prize winners are another source of pride, and rightly so. An extraordinary amount of Nobel Prize winners are Jewish. It is said that 22 percent (or 197) of all Nobel Prize winners between 1901 and 2016 were/are Jewish, and considering that only 0.2 percent of the world population is Jewish, that is really quite something. However, it must be noted that not all of those people would be considered Jewish religiously. While the majority of those 197 people were

Jewish, a good number of them were/are half or three-quarter Jews, according to one source.[104]

The *Jewish Virtual Library* also uses the figure of 22 percent but lists the recipients with asterisks beside the names of those who had a Jewish father but a non-Jewish mother.[105]

Other articles will specify that 20-22 percent of recipients were Jewish or of Jewish heritage.

The point is that Jewish heritage comes into play when an accomplishment is a source of pride. Half-Jews are counted as Jews by some if they won a Nobel Prize. For example, Douglas D. Osheroff won the Nobel Prize for Physics in 1996. His biography at Nobelprize.org begins:

"Ethnically, I come from a mixed family. My father was the son of Jewish immigrants who left Russia shortly after the turn of the century, and my mother was the daughter of a Lutheran minister whose parents were from what is now Slovakia."[106]

That sounds a bit like my own background, the paternal side at least. But Osheroff is counted as a part of that 22 percent of Jewish winners. I wonder how many times he's heard the ol', "If your mother's a Jew..." Or was he ever called a goy?

Don't get me wrong—I think Half-Jews should be counted in these lists. What I want to point out is the hypocrisy of accepting Half-Jews when it's convenient but leaving us out in the cold other times.

In this case, the Jewish ethnic ancestry is important, and in fact, according to a Pew Study, 55 percent of Israeli Jews and 62 percent of American Jews believe that being Jewish is mainly a matter of ancestry or culture. Only 22 percent of Israeli Jews and 15 percent of American Jews thought it was strictly about religion, while less than a quarter of both Israeli and American Jews considered it to be about both religion and ancestry/culture.[107]

So most Jews themselves feel that being Jewish is about ancestry, more so than religion. If that's the case, why deny Half-Jews their right to be Jewish when they share in the very same ancestry? The Holocaust happened to our ancestors as well. The Russian pogroms. The European Inquisitions. The slaughter of Jews scapegoated for the Black Plague, and the ethnic cleansing of Jews from Arab countries in 1948 and beyond. These are our ancestors too. And aren't we cousins? No more distant than 30th cousins to be exact. If one's Jewishness is more about ancestry than religion, Half-Jews cannot be discounted because scientifically speaking, ancestry does not merely come through the mother's lineage.

The same Pew study found that 71 percent of Israeli Jews believe a person can be Jewish even as an Atheist. What's more, 52 percent of the Haredim, the religious Jews, express the same opinion.[108] And only 5 percent of the Haredim agree that people converted by a non-Orthodox rabbi are Jewish, while 19 percent of the same religious Jews believe that people can still be Jewish even if they believe that Jesus is the Messiah. That is actually 1 percent more than how Israeli Jews as a whole, spanning from secular to religious, answered the same question.[109]

So, as I stated in an earlier chapter, Jews who converted via a Reform, Conservative or any other rabbi besides Orthodox, are not considered Jewish, especially by the Haredim in Israel. Far more Haredim believe that Jews are still Jews, even if they think that Jesus is their savior, (thereby making them Christian religiously speaking), and if a Jew does not believe in the existence of God, he's still a Jew.

By contrast, only 11 percent of Israeli Muslims and 14 percent of Israeli Christians answered that a person could be Muslim or Christian, respectively, without believing in God.[110] This demonstrates that the Jewish identity is far more complex than the identity of other religions. Islam and

Christianity are religions, but Jews are indeed an ethnoreligious group.

Half-Jews are a part of that "ethno."

And yet, this ever important "mother rule" has become so powerful, that many American Jewish girls in the younger generation have a flippant attitude about marrying a Jew. In this case, I have no statistics to back up my statement. All I can say is that I've heard this more than once, that American Jewish girls know their children will be Jewish no matter what because of matrilineage, and therefore, there is no need to find a Jewish husband. They can marry whomever they want.

Men, on the other hand, must find that Jewish wife in order to have Jewish children.

Another reason people sometimes give for this "mother rule" is that the mother is far more influential in the religious upbringing of the children than the father. People who say this obviously didn't know my father.

Christianity was banned in my household growing up. My mother was not allowed to attend church, and only when my father said no to Christmas did my mother put her foot down. She insisted we at least celebrate the commercial aspect of the holiday, and my father acquiesced, understanding the importance of that to her.

It meant presents and an artificial Christmas tree (but no lights, he demanded). Somehow, my mother was also able to slip in Easter baskets in the spring, so to us, Christianity was Santa Claus and the Easter Bunny. But there were no Easter egg hunts, and we never watched any Christmas movies either. As for the true meanings of these holidays, I knew that Christmas was Jesus' birthday, but I never understood what Easter was all about until decades later when I discovered that Easter is actually a far more important religious holiday than Christmas. Who would have guessed?

One thing that had always bothered me was that I was missing out on all the Christian stuff my friends did with their families. Knowing I was half and half and living in a Christian country—no, it is not a Christian theocracy but is most definitely a Christian-majority nation with Christian Bible-reading forefathers and Christmas decorations practically in every store and on every Main Street in every town during the month of December—I was jealous of my friends who got to experience a real Christmas. It was a mystery to me. What went on in these Christian homes over the holidays? What was it like to go to Midnight Mass on Christmas Eve?

Admittedly, I did get a taste of it. We had that artificial Christmas tree and decorated it with some of my German grandmother's old ornaments and some new ones too. We opened presents on Christmas morning but had to wait for my parents to come down mid-morning, then have breakfast and then finally open the gifts late morning. It was like torture for us, but my father didn't understand Christmas himself or how other families went about it. He probably thought we were lucky to get any Christmas at all and should be thankful, late morning or not.

In grade school I was in the school chorus. How that happened I have no idea since I can't carry a tune, but I suppose my voice was a little better back then, good enough to sing in a group. We would sing Christmas carols for the Christmas concert in December, which I guess these days is usually called a "Winter Concert" to appease those who are offended at the majority-Christian population assuming everyone else is Christian too. When I was younger, it used to bother me until I realized it's not a big deal, and we do live in a democracy where majority rules. I have no problem with well-wishers saying "Merry Christmas" to everyone instead of "Happy Holidays" because they mean well, and what difference does it make? They're not purposely trying to offend anyone. Quite the opposite actually.

One aspect of Christmas I'll always remember is going shopping with my dad for my mom's gift. Each year, he'd wait until close to the very day itself to take me out and find something for her. We'd go to the beautifully decorated mall, which was already a madhouse by then, and get shoved around in the stores where there was little room to breathe, let alone take the time to look at things. People would cut in line to check out first, and it left a bad taste in my mouth, realizing Christmas for them was a selfish affair.

Still, there was something special about going somewhere alone with my dad, just the two of us. It hardly ever happened. We'd pick out a gift and go to the "Jewish ladies" to get it professionally gift-wrapped. That's how we worded it. You see, there was always a table set up at the mall with a group of Jewish women who would wrap gifts. I have no idea if they were raising money for a synagogue or for a Jewish charity because I was too young to pay attention to such details. I only knew that my father wanted to go to the table of the Jewish ladies, and it became a Christmas tradition for us—just my dad and I, shopping for my mom and ending the evening by supporting Jews. It's a perfect example of growing up interfaith.

Though Christmas held only a small place in our lives, Easter held next to nothing. That holiday was a true enigma. What was this Easter egg hunt that my friends did? And they painted eggs? Why weren't we allowed to do that? And they got pretty dresses and went to church? What was that like? It all looked so beautiful and spring-like.

One time my father did allow me to go to my friend's house for an Easter egg hunt, but he asked a lot of questions and wasn't at all happy about it. It was the one and only time I partook in those festivities, but now, as an adult, I get it. My father knew what Easter was, and out of all the Christian holidays, none conflict more with Judaism than that one. The "Jews killed Jesus" accusation began there. Of course I didn't understand any of these things as a child. All I knew was that my friends were Christian and doing fun stuff that we weren't allowed to do.

Understanding religion based on the bits and pieces I got growing up was like trying to put together a puzzle, but nevertheless there was a yearning for it, a deep desire for spirituality and truth.

I later learned far more about Christianity from my childhood best friend, a born-again Christian. Well, that's what they used to call them. Now I suppose they're Evangelicals, but however you want to label her, she was religious. And she always tried to pull me over to her side, but I blocked those attempts, putting up a wall when it came to that because I was brought up to resist such things. But I wondered. What if she's right? What if Jesus really is the Messiah? She's smart, extremely smart in fact. And she's a logical thinker. And, and... good things happen to her. She says her prayers are answered. Is that because she prays to Jesus? So what if I'm wrong, and she's right? What if, this lack of religion has created a void that needs to be filled? And what should fill it?

Judaism or Christianity?

I really wanted to fill the void with Judaism. At Syracuse, I began visiting a rabbi, who provided me with reading material. I'd go over it with him, ask him questions, and he'd answer. But then something happened. He told me I absolutely had to get in touch with my Jewish relatives. I knew it was an impossibility. My father had cut himself and us off from his family, and there was no way he would have allowed me to contact them, nor did I know how to reach them, even if I'd wanted.

What I did instead was make an announcement to my father. "You always said that when we turn 18, we can decide what religion we want to follow. Well, I'm 18, and I choose Judaism."

I thought he'd be happy, flattered that between his religion and my mother's Catholicism, I'd chosen his—that with all the religions in the world, the various Christian denominations, Judaism, Buddhism, Hinduism or Islam (okay, the last three were unlikely considering where and how I was raised, but still!), I'd decided that his religion was the right one for me. He should have been ecstatic at such a declaration from his daughter, right? Wrong.

He was angry and started going on about what if I'm wearing a Star of David, and some guy who would otherwise have asked me out doesn't once he sees that. "Why would I want to go out with someone like that anyway?" I asked him. Besides, I already had a Star of David necklace, and Judaism was rooted inside me, inherited somehow, genetically or spiritually, passed down and innate, natural.

He just hemmed and hawed. He really had no answer for me, no reason as to why it upset him. In fact, he even said that although he wasn't a fan of organized religion, if anyone's got it right, it's the Jews. So why then? What's the problem? To this day, I have no idea.

After my father passed away, my mother told me that near the end of his life, he lamented that not one of his children married a Jew. I was absolutely shocked. Not once did he express that desire to me, nor did he ever encourage us in any way. Quite the contrary, actually. And he himself didn't marry a Jew. Perhaps he was beginning to feel guilty that the Jewish line ended with him.

Between his nonsensical reaction, the rabbi's demands (maybe not demands exactly, but that's how I saw it), and my Jewish friend calling me a goy, I shut down my quest and pulled myself out of the path I was on to Judaism. *Forget them,* I thought. *They don't want me.*

During my final year at Syracuse, I did begin taking a Jewish history course as an elective. The first week, I realized this elective was requiring about 400 pages of reading in one week, and at that point I was deep into my major, needing all my concentration on the important courses required to graduate, which also carried a heavy workload including a considerable amount of reading. No matter how much I wanted to study Jewish history, it was an elective. I had to drop it. The books I kept though, reading them in my own time.

Years passed by, and I was as confused as ever. I always loved the Jewish people but still had it in my head they didn't want me.

Eventually I met my husband, who was raised Catholic, and we started our family. And I knew, raising children without religion and allowing them to decide as adults without any spiritual guidance, may be the worst thing parents can do. They say that children raised this way tend to pick no religion at all. Based on my personal experience, raised with this mindset, I would have to say that children need some sort of direction, or else they will be confused their entire lives.

Susan Katz Miller, the author of *Being Both: Embracing Two Religions in One Interfaith Family*, makes a case for raising children from an interfaith marriage with both religions. Conducting a survey of parents who were a part of interfaith communities, providing their children with a religious education encompassing more than one religion, Katz Miller found this to be a positive approach. Neither parent's religious background was left out, encouraging family unity and less confusion for the children.[111]

Katz Miller, like me, was a patrilineal Jewish child, and as such, she's well-acquainted with the "if your mother's a Jew..." rule. Though raised as a Reform Jew, she cannot be considered a Jew, even by all Reform rabbis, because some accept patrilineage while others don't.

Interfaith relationships are quite common these days. A Pew study from October 2016, found that 1 in 5 American adults were raised in interfaith homes.[112] Many of them, however, were raised by two Christian parents, one Catholic and one Protestant. Another 12 percent were raised by one religious parent and one parent who was Atheist, Agnostic or nothing specific. The same study found that adults who do not identify with a particular religion were raised either by a parent or parents who were not affiliated with a specific religion themselves. A total of 62 percent of the "religious nones" had been raised with no religion.[113] They had no guidance, and they grew up to choose nothing.

This data supports the suggestion by religious authorities that interfaith couples who raise their children without religion, as my parents did, telling them to choose when they reach the age of 18, are making a mistake. Without spiritual guidance and a sense of direction, why would they choose anything?

One thing I can say, I was raised with a strong set of values. Morality was big in my household, along with a good work ethic, and the importance of education was stressed. Was there some hypocrisy that went along with the lessons we were taught? Isn't there always? At least we knew right from wrong and how to be good people.

The cultural aspect of being Jewish was most apparent. We sure didn't eat kosher, but we did enjoy lox and bagels, whitefish, gefilte fish and a family favorite, fried matzah (also known as matzah brei). We carried the devastation of the Holocaust in our hearts and cheered for Israel, proud of her accomplishments and strength.

But after my college experiences, I didn't see how I would be accepted, and I was no authority on Judaism in terms of teaching the religion to my offspring. At the same time, my upbringing led me to the conclusion that children need religion in their lives. Many won't agree with that statement, and there are valid complaints about organized religion. There is hypocrisy in probably every religion. There are insincere people, and there are cases spanning across various religions of abuse of power, sexual misconduct, even pedophilia. And there are questionable manmade rules, at times a lack of spirituality replaced with memorized prayers and rituals people race through as routine, without stopping to think about what it is they are doing or saying. Some believe that people who aren't religious are more caring. In fact, there was a study done with those very same findings: nonreligious people are more empathetic and altruistic than the religious.[114]

I, however, wanted to give whatever children I would have the religious guidance I never got. My husband felt the same way. So what did we do?

First stop, the Catholic Church.

Catholicism

My husband was Catholic, as was my mother, so I began thinking about my best friend growing up and all her answered prayers. The thing is, however I felt about Catholicism, I still saw it as better than no religion at all.

The priest at our local Catholic Church was nothing like what I'd imagined a priest to be. He was from Ireland and was hilarious. Sometimes he would even say, "Oh my God," during his sermons. A priest! I asked him, "Isn't that taking the Lord's name in vain?" He said it wasn't, with a reasoning that made sense at the time.

Unfortunately, while some of my anxiety about church was quieted by an unexpected priest, there were other issues. Since I wasn't Catholic, I couldn't take communion. That was awkward. There are two main reasons why people don't take communion: one, they committed some horrible sin and haven't yet confessed; two, they aren't Catholic. They could also be divorced, but it seems nowadays that doesn't deter people from taking communion.

Because of these rules, when I would stay in the pews and let the people next to me pass by, I would get odd looks, judgmental stares. The priest told me, "Don't worry what they think. Most of those people are bigger sinners than you'll ever be. Who are they to judge you?"

I liked this guy.

He also provided me with a solution: "Just go up with everyone else, and when it's your turn and you come up to me, just cross your arms over your chest and look down before walking away. No one will realize you didn't take communion."

I tried it, and yes, it worked. Regardless, I always knew I was an outsider there. I was no Catholic. Likeable priest or not, I stuck out like a sore thumb—well, I felt like I did anyway.

Still, I was willing to try. As I had been briefly married before (a big mistake, but let's not get into that), I'd need an annulment. The wait time for an annulment was expected to be about two years.

That's two years of waiting to annul my first marriage, despite being divorced and remarried for at least another two or three years already. And then, once this annulment would take place, I'd have to remarry my current husband in the church. Until that time, although we were legally married, in the eyes of the church, we were shacking up together.

The bureaucracy was just too much for me. An annulment over a divorce is just semantics and a long, unnecessary process. Is this really what God requires? Or is it just human nonsense? No offense to my Catholic readers, but it wasn't for me.

Nondenominational Protestantism

Time went on, and we revisited the subject of religion. It was a topic that would never completely go away because I knew the importance and didn't want my indecision to lead us down the same path as my parents, raising their children without religious guidance. I talked to that old Evangelical childhood friend of mine, and she made it her mission to find a church for us, a nondenominational church.

At this time, we were living in the Bible Belt. My husband is from a foreign country, and I am a Yankee from New Jersey. In this small town, we were both outsiders who didn't fit in with the locals born and raised there. While some were super friendly, other people in places like this put up a front of that stereotypical Southern hospitality and Southern charm, but the reality is, without having grown up there and without being a member of their church, outsiders aren't often fully embraced and welcomed to their inner circles. Luckily, we had befriended a local family who wasn't like that, and through our jobs, we'd met more friends, mostly outsiders like us.

But I always knew, I was different.

From afar, my childhood friend found a church that checked off all her boxes, so we decided to try it. Maybe we could join this Bible Belt culture of going to church on Sundays, but more than anything it was about our little one and providing that religious guidance.

Arriving at the church, a nervousness overcame me, but my husband was there to hold my hand, as I was there to hold his. A greeter at the door put us at ease, smiling and introducing himself, guiding us inside. There was a nursery, or children's church, which was important to us because what kid wants to be bored to tears, sitting with the adults? And toddlers won't sit still anyway, so without this, we wouldn't even have attempted it.

The music thumped loudly, a band rocking out contemporary Christian music, rather than old-fashioned hymns, with relatable lyrics, soulful and spiritual. The lead singer's voice had a sort of raspy quality to it, raspy yet beautiful at the same time, and he poured out his heart as he sung, moving me to tears at times. He was a young guy, younger than us. All the musicians were. And they were as good as famous recording artists, better than most in fact. If I were to say who my favorite singer is, it would probably be this guy, an unknown.

Eventually, the music had to end, so the pastor could deliver his sermon. He was another young guy, older than us, but funny, good-looking and cool.

My husband and I found this church to be different from anything we'd ever expected or experienced and decided to continue visiting on Sundays.

Over time, we met more and more people, and we began attending Bible studies. I'd call my childhood friend to ask questions and discuss what verses meant, and we became closer than ever.

Still, I knew I was an outsider, a pretender somehow.

Time went on, and things started falling apart at this church. Disagreements over how things were run combined with a newcomer who'd already had the intention of starting his own church, led to its downfall. Many people joined the church planter, who was even cooler and hipper than the first pastor. He was an outsider too. Actually most of the people from these two churches had come from either the Northeast or Florida.

The new pastor was a good businessman and excellent marketer. He knew how to get things done, how to raise money and how to attract people to this young and vibrant church. Humor was a great quality he possessed, and his sermons were probably at times, funnier than those of the other guy. He'd use relatable circumstances to make his case, while preaching from the Bible at the same time. There were no religious rules, just the Word of God, as it's called.

We became friends with the pastor and his wife, along with many of the other churchgoers. I volunteered at the nursery, while my husband volunteered to join the cleaning crew.

During this time, we'd also visited a neighbor's church and continued attending Bible studies. Suddenly, we knew lots of people and were a part of a "tribe" of sorts.

Yet something kept nagging at me. Not everything added up. Some verses contradicted others, and when I would ask questions, no one had an acceptable answer. The explanations would only go so far until reaching that wall of, "That's where faith comes in."

Faith works if it makes sense. Where is the logic of 1+1=3?

My husband had the same doubts, but we wanted to be faithful.

When the housing market crashed, we were affected like most people. I realized how depressed I was in this place, where I would forever be an outsider. How could I ever fit in when I wasn't born or raised there? And Christianity? It's a nice religion, but I was the oddball Jewish girl, whose heart was with my people. I didn't grow up with Christianity, and it never felt right to me. As much as I tried, and I really did, deeply immersing myself in this church culture, it wasn't me.

Nothing could describe it better than that Jason Segel quote: "At Christian school you're the Jewish kid, and at Hebrew school you're the Christian kid... I decided at that point, like OK, it's me versus the world kind of."[115]

Yeah. Me versus the world, or rather, my husband and I as a team against the world.

These Christian friends were wonderful, but the problem was within myself. I know I'm a Jew, not a Christian. The mustard seed didn't take; it had fallen along the rocks.[116]

The time was right to leave. We'd briefly lived out West before, and I'd always wanted to return. After much discussion and planning, my husband and I made the decision to move across the country. It wasn't an easy transition, but it was the right move. No longer were we outsiders because there is so much diversity here, and many residents are originally from somewhere else.

Believe it or not, we again got involved with local churches. They were nice, but they weren't the same. The worst part was that my attempts to keep in touch with the church friends from back East were futile. Out of sight, out of mind. I began wondering what the point was to these friendships if they were based solely on belonging to the same church and nothing more. After all, shouldn't these relationships be strong enough to endure a move? My friendship with my childhood best friend always lasted no matter where we lived.

Then other issues started, and my disappointment in people led me to reevaluate things. Again, my husband and I discussed inconsistencies we saw in Scripture, at least, as we perceived it. To be clear, I'm not telling my story to offend anyone or any religion, and people can make convincing cases for various religions, including Christianity.

As for the people, nobody's perfect, so we really need to focus on God and on what we believe. I kept getting pulled back to Judaism. No matter how much I adored my Christian friends, the Jewish voice inside me grew stronger, telling me I'm different, and I don't fit in at church. Something was amiss, and I realized that one of the biggest draws to the church for me was the music. It brought me closer to God via spiritual lyrics and music that resonated with me, in a genre that was my taste. But that's just music, isn't it? What about truth?

Another benefit to church was community, being a part of something. The trouble is that I always knew I was an outsider. A Half-Jew.

Judaism

Our church days ended, and I immersed myself in research for my book and fighting the Jew-bashers and Israel haters online. My research included Judaism itself, and I learned things I'd never known before. Now I was reading both Christian and Jewish apologetics and understood each point of view. Everything started to make sense.

Again, my objective here is not to offend any Christian readers or argue Scripture, and so I won't go into specifics. All I will say is that in Judaism, there is a logic to most issues, the "mother law" notwithstanding. And it felt right. Jews are my people, and this is where I belong, whether I'm wanted or not.

Love for Israel

One thing that never confused me was my deep love for and inherent connection to the Jewish State. As an Ashkenazi, I know that Israel is my ancestral homeland. Once upon a time, if you go back far enough, most Jewish families came from Israel, and my family is no different. I share the same history with those allowed to call themselves Jewish. In other words, Jewish history is my history. Abraham, Isaac and Jacob are my ancestors, every bit as much as they are the ancestors of someone considered Jewish. When my father married a Christian, that did not erase the family history, nor did it erase the persecution my Jewish ancestors endured over the course of thousands of years. It also did not erase the anti-Semitism thrown the way of my father, grandparents, great-grandparents and on and on. And of course it is not all about suffering but about family history and the blood running through our veins.

As an ethnoreligious group, the Jewish identity is a complicated one. Whereas someone with an Italian father is allowed to feel a connection to "the motherland," in this case, Italy, someone with a Jewish father but non-Jewish mother is not called a Jew and is therefore made to feel that there cannot possibly be an innate connection to the Jewish homeland.

What is passed through the veins remains in the veins. Labels do not alter the ancestry or DNA make-up of a human being. Blood may be a taboo word in relation to Jews, but we have blood like anyone else and Half-Jews feel our fathers' blood no less than our mothers'. Though it may not be true for all of us, for many, a connection to Israel is rooted deep inside us. Call it blood, call it innate, or call it whatever you want. But it's there.

As far as I know, there has not been a study dedicated to Half-Jews and their support or lack thereof for Israel. With that said, it has been my experience that a large number of Half-Jews are as supportive or even more supportive of the Jewish State as their fully Jewish counterparts.

In Pew Research Center's 2013 "A Portrait of Jewish Americans," 69 percent of American Jews said they were emotionally attached to Israel. In the same survey, 87 percent stated that caring about Israel was either an important or essential part of being Jewish.[117]

How Is the Jewish Identity Defined?

The Pew study found that out of the U.S. adult Jewish population that year, 78 percent were Jews by religion, while 22 percent were Jews of no religion—Jews of no religion, but still Jews. In this study, 62 percent of American Jews believed that being Jewish was more a matter of ancestry and culture; only 15 percent believed it was a matter of religion alone; and 23 percent felt it was a combination of ancestry, culture and religion.[118] That's really quite something. Imagine, six out of ten Jews did not see the religion itself as having much importance to the Jewish identity.

The study broke it down even further. Out of those Jews who considered themselves to be Jewish by religion, 55 percent still saw their Jewishness as a matter of ancestry and culture, rather than religion. Out of the Jews who had no religion, 83 percent answered that being Jewish was mainly a matter of ancestry and culture. That one makes sense. They aren't religious, but they're still Jews and don't want to lose that.[119]

The same study also provides insight regarding interfaith marriages between Jews and non-Jewish spouses. It is no surprise that the Jews who are not religious are more likely to marry a non-Jewish spouse: 79 percent in fact. And in those interfaith marriages, 45 percent are either raising their children Jewish or partly Jewish, religiously speaking.[120]

Many Israeli Jews worry over American Jews taking assimilation too far because of the apparent loss of the Jewish identity and importance of religion in their lives. One thing's for sure, intermarriage is becoming more common as time goes on.

When my parents married in 1967, they had to marry in secret, eloping at the courthouse. In those days, this inter-marriage was as controversial as an interracial marriage. My German grandparents didn't want their daughter marrying a Jew, and my Jewish grandparents wanted their son to marry a fellow Jew because marrying within the religion as well as within the Jewish ethnicity is how Jews have maintained their identity for thousands of years. Otherwise, they would have disappeared amongst the oceans of other people, just as many other ethnicities and cultures have assimilated completely and been fully absorbed by those around them.

The Pew study reports interesting numbers. Among American Jews who have married a non-Jewish spouse, 17 percent had married before 1970, like my own parents. The percentages gradually increase as the years pass. The interfaith couples who married between 1970 and 1974 rose to 35 percent, more than doubling the numbers from the previous grouping. In the 1980s, it increased to 42 percent, then to 55 percent in the late 1990s, and up to 58 percent in the 2000's up through 2013, the year of the survey.[121]

Obviously, this demonstrates how much more accepted interfaith relationships are now as compared to back when my parents married, but it also shows that assimilation. Does it affect anything?

Well, 94 percent of American Jews are still proud to be Jewish. Three-quarters have a strong sense of belonging to the Jewish people. And as for Israel, seven out of ten Jews feel an attachment to the Jewish State.[122]

The Significance of Israel

But why is support for Israel important anyway? The basic answer is quite simple: Israel is the one and only Jewish State. Before the rebirth of Israel, the creation of the modern state in 1948, Jews had no homeland. Stuck in Diaspora and living amongst people who hated them, they were subject to discrimination, persecution and ultimately, genocide. If Israel had existed during World War II, there would have been no Holocaust.

While there were efforts to escape German-occupied Europe, only around 16,000 Jews were able to flee to Palestine between 1937 and 1944, with the help of the Zionist movement.[123] At that time, however, the land was governed under the British Mandate, and the British had restricted Jewish immigration but did not restrict Arab immigration.[124] There were few options for Jews to find refuge. Largely denied entry to Palestine, some Jews managed to escape to other parts of Europe or Asia, but their numbers were few compared to the six million who perished. Every imaginable obstacle was in their way, as they were subject to the laws of others who had little or no compassion. Without their own state, Jews were denied the right to exist.

Now, Israel is the Jewish State, but it is also Jews' ancestral homeland. In the Torah, God gave the land to Abraham, Isaac and Jacob and to their descendants. If you don't buy that, you can read the history books.

An article entitled, "We Never Left: The Jews' Continuous Presence in the Land of Israel," written by Lee S. Bender and Jerome R. Verlin, provides an easy summary of the Jewish history in the Holy Land. Jews maintained a presence during the Talmudic Age, the Muslim Dynasties, the Crusader Rule, the Mamluks, and 400 years of Ottoman Turk rule.[125]

Additionally, in his overview of Jewish history in the land, Jerrold L. Sobel writes of the nearly 4000-year history in Israel, reminding readers in a slightly more detailed analysis than Bender and Verlin of the constant Jewish presence. From the biblical patriarchs to David and Solomon to the time of the Romans and up through today, Jews have never completely left. "Despite massacres, pogroms, expulsions, and forced conversions, Jews have dwelled in their capital, Jerusalem, and surrounding cities and towns such as Hebron, Nablus, and Jericho since time immemorial," Sobel explains.[126]

What's more, there has been a continuous Jewish presence from biblical times in the four holy cities of Judaism: Jerusalem, Hebron, Safed and Tiberias.[127]

Jerusalem, the eternal capital, is at the heart of Judaism and what it means to be Jewish. Sobel writes, "For those Jews forced into exile throughout the world, one theme has remained constant: the dream of returning to their homeland, Eretz Yisrael, to rebuild and restore her to the glory of old. Throughout the millennia, Diaspora Jews to this day face towards Jerusalem during prayers."[128]

"Next year in Jerusalem" is how Jews end the Passover seder, and Israeli Prime Minister Benjamin Netanyahu stressed the importance of Jerusalem when he explained in a speech for Jerusalem Day that the words "Jerusalem" and "Zion" are mentioned in the Hebrew Bible 850 times.[129]

From both a religious standpoint and from the cultural and historical perspective of a people and their land, Jerusalem and Israel as a whole, are inarguably the "motherland" to all Jews around the world. And I, as an Ashkenazi, feel it.

Is it innate? It seems to be, in my case at least. If I'd been half Jewish ethnically but fully Jewish through my mother's line, this innate love for Israel would never be questioned. But since I'm Jewish through the wrong half, making me, in the eyes of many, not Jewish at all, proclaiming my inherent love for Israel may be appreciated but not accepted in the same way as if it had come from "a real Jew." This is something I've experienced myself but is reaffirmed by others.

On the other hand, Israeli Jews tend to be more forgiving of that tiny detail. A 57 year-old half Jewish European named Marc,[130] now living in the U.S., has spent some time in the Holy Land. When I asked how he feels about Israel, this is what he told me:

"Having been born and grown up in Germany, I could tell Jews need a homeland because anti-Semitism really never stopped. Though, for the most part, Jews have been safe in Germany since 1945, but it has gotten worse since the '90s. Because my father is Jewish, I felt an immediate kinship to Israel, and after volunteering in a kibbutz for six months in 1983, I became even more resolved to stand up for Israel when false accusations were thrown."

Marc explained that as a Half-Jew, he felt rejected by some Jews but not by most. He found Israeli Jews to be more accepting.

"For me, it was far different. After pointing out that I am half Jewish, it made no difference to them. One Israeli even told me that I should tell German Jews they are full of it for treating me differently. I was astonished by the acceptance in Israel."

But how did Marc's love for Israel come to be? Was he raised in the synagogue? Was it innate?

"I was not raised religious at all. My parents decided I should make my own decision when I am an adult. That may be why I am not religious."

Sounds familiar.

"I don't think I was born with an attachment to Israel. It was a gradual experience while being a child. We went often to the Jewish community center which organized many events during the '60s, and it helped that my city's Jewish community of about 1500 was fairly small and close."

I've also had Israelis tell me I'm Jewish, while American Jews are less likely to agree.

Either way, Israel is an important part of the Jewish identity. The Pew study found that 43 percent of American Jews consider "caring about Israel" to be an essential part of being Jewish. Most essential, however, is remembering the Holocaust, followed by leading an ethical and moral life, working for justice/equality, being intellectually curious, having a good sense of humor, and being a part of the Jewish community. At the very bottom were the least essential aspects of being Jewish: Only 19 percent said "observing Jewish law," and 14 percent said "eating Jewish foods."[131]

Many of us can check the most important boxes, but what is interesting to me is how far down the list observing Jewish law is. Considering the priority of the "mother rule," one would think the rest of Jewish law would be equally essential. On the contrary, it would seem according to these findings, that while the mother rule immediately flies out of the mouths of Jews when dealing with Half-Jews, the rest of Jewish law takes a backseat.

To reiterate that point, only 55 percent of American Jews answered that religion is either very or somewhat important in their lives, compared to 79 percent of the U.S. general public. Furthermore, 23 percent of the Jews questioned were Atheists. Another interesting statistic is that only 22 percent kept kosher at home. [132]

But that mother rule...

Jewish mother or not, I love Israel, and I'm not the only Half-Jew who feels that way.

Law of Return

The Law of Return gives every Jew in Diaspora the right to immigrate to Israel. "Immigrate" is actually the wrong word because Jews are already a part of the Jewish Nation, and therefore, when a Jew immigrates to the Holy Land, he is returning to his ancestral homeland. Rather than "immigrating" or "emigrating" to Israel, he is "making aliyah," or ascending, going up, in a spiritual sense.[133] One who makes aliyah is not an immigrant but an "oleh," which translates as "one who goes up."

This law was passed by the Knesset, the Israeli parliament, in 1950, and in it, "Jew" is defined as someone with a Jewish mother or someone who has converted but is not a member of another religion.[134]

An amendment passed in 1970 to include family members of Jews: spouses, children and grandchildren of Jews, and the spouses of the children and grandchildren. This means that any Half-Jew or even quarter-Jew can apply, although it does not make them Jewish by Halakhah. In other words, religiously speaking, they will not be considered Jewish, but they are Jewish enough to make aliyah.

So I qualify.

The reasoning behind the amendment is said to be that if someone is Jewish enough for the Nazis, Jewish enough to be persecuted, that person is Jewish enough for the Law of Return.[135]

The Mischlinge

I happen to be a mischling,[136] mixed blood. This was the legal German term for people having both Aryan and Jewish blood in Nazi Germany. The Nuremberg Laws of 1935 declared a Jew to be anyone with at least three Jewish grandparents. They could be practicing another religion, but they were Jews regardless. People like me with two Jewish grandparents were Jews if they were practicing Judaism or were married to Jews. Otherwise, they were mischlinge of the first degree. Mischlinge of the second degree meant one Jewish grandparent. The Nazis were methodical in their specific classification, to say the least.

The fate of the mischlinge depended upon their appearance. If they looked like Jews, they could be treated like Jews, regardless of their mischling status. "Acting" like Jews could also get them thrown in the heap with the rest, and of course these things were purely subjective. If they were Half-Jews like me and were spared, they were supposed to be sterilized, according to what was decided at the Wannsee Conference in 1942, where the details for The Final Solution were hashed out. The mischlinge of the second degree were considered Germans for the most part, but again, if they looked Jewish, all bets were off. The laws were strict but seemed to have enough leeway for Nazis to examine mischlinge on a case-by-case basis, and if you didn't fit into their idea of the perfect race, they could make that determination. Either way, mischlinge must have lived in fear, and many perished along with those who fit the full-blown Nazi classification of a Jew.

One way or another, I would have faced discrimination and walked on eggshells as a mischling in Nazi Germany. If I looked Jewish in their minds, I could have been sent to a concentration or death camp, and based on my appearance, the odds would not have been in my favor. This is something I've thought about throughout my life—I could have been sent to the ovens had I lived in that place and time. And it does affect me. I feel solidarity with those who are allowed to call themselves Jews.

Identifying with Our Ancestors

This is not a sympathy plea, oh woe is me, because I am fortunate enough that I do not live in that place and time. On the contrary, I live in one of the greatest nations on earth, and I suppose that anyone could really cry over their ancestors and what they went through: African Americans and slavery; Hindus and Sikhs and the Islamic conquest of India; Native Americans and the Indian wars. The list could go on and on.

But everyone identifies more closely with their own families, ancestors and ethnic groups and their hardships. We may have compassion for anyone suffering, but it really hits home when it becomes more personal. That's one aspect of genealogy that comes through loud and clear. When those searching for answers find them and discover what their grandparents, great-grandparents, etc., had to endure, and especially when it was a famous or infamous part of history, it will affect them on an emotional level, far more deeply than a vague account written by and about people with whom there is no obvious connection.

If you read about the Jamestown settlement, it's interesting. But if you discover that one of your relatives was there, it's something else. The same goes for triumphs. The Underground Railroad was quite something, but if your relative was one of the people taking those risks to save others, it means that much more.

The Salem witch trials? The Civil War? The Puritans? Now what about Abraham, Isaac and Jacob from the Torah? Of course that's going far back, but think of the Holocaust. There aren't many survivors left, but there are some. It was recent enough that my parents were born just before the war ended. And I know that those victims were my people. It doesn't matter if they're my people on my father's side, my mother's side or both. What difference does that make? No one discounts their ancestors on one side of the family or the other. We are descended from the people on both sides.

The Nazis, on the other hand, I could do without.

The Holocaust was a systematic genocide, with the ultimate goal of obliterating an entire people, my people. And where my Jewish family came from was one of the worst places for Jews during the war. In that region of the world, entire villages were taken to the woods, stripped naked and shot down. It brings tears to my eyes just thinking about it, how others could not see their humanity.

Unfortunately, the idea of "half-breeds" not being the same as others who are full-blooded this or that, is not confined to Jews. Personally, I have biracial friends who are not enough of each race to fit in with one or the other. Either their skin is too light or too dark, their hair is too curly or not curly enough, or they're perceived as having an advantage over others either financially or because of the way they look or whatever other excuse people come up with. On the other side, they may have a disadvantage. They are half this and half that, but they're neither, nor.

This idea carries through to people who are only one ethnicity but have moved to another land. For example, Mexicans living in the United States are seen as rich Americans by their friends and family back home. They're still Mexican, but now something's changed; they're different. Yet in America, they're Mexican. In Iran, Persian Americans have been accused of spying. They're Persian, but they're American, leading to suspicion by the paranoid.

Yet Jews are Jews no matter where in the world they live. Jewish ancestry, culture and religion is the common denominator for all Jews in Diaspora. With that said, not every Jew agrees politically, and in fact, there is a running joke: two Jews, three opinions.

This also applies to Israel. There are Jews against the State of Israel, groups who even protest alongside others who support Palestinian terrorism. No one ever says they aren't real Jews, but there is another name that sometimes comes up: "Erev Rav."

Erev Rav and Kapos

This term is loosely thrown around to call someone a traitor. When it comes to the anti-Israel haters, it may be appropriate. However, some will use it to describe secular Jews while others will call mixed Jews like me Erev Rav. They have no idea what it really means.

According to Rabbi Kenneth Cohen, a Torah instructor in Jerusalem, the Erev Rav were the mixed multitude who left Egypt with the Hebrews. He writes in an article posted on *The Times of Israel* website, that they were "insincere Egyptian converts" responsible for all the complaining that went on while the Jews wandered in the desert, as well as for the Golden Calf.[137] [138]

Cohen explains that the Erev Rav are said to exist in every generation, but the Erev Rav today are probably not the actual descendants of those Egyptian converts. He calls it "spiritual pollution," the souls of those traitors placed in others, and he describes them, not as people simply disagreeing over politics but as Jews who are against their brethren, people who are more interested in other nations than in the Jewish Nation.[139]

The Erev Rav can be completely Jewish ethnically, but they are not loyal to their people. This has nothing to do with mischlinge or Half-Jews but has everything to do with the heart.

"Kapo" is another word to describe Jews who work against fellow Jews. In the concentration camps in Nazi Germany, there were Jewish prisoners with supervisory positions who often treated the other prisoners just as despicably as the S.S. They may have been doing it to win favor, but they were more like traitors, even if they were also prisoners.

With an elevated status, these Jews, called kapos, worked to improve their own lives while hurting their brethren.

In today's society, kapos may be like the Erev Rav, except that the term "kapo" is used, not on Half-Jews, but on Jews who are anti-Israel, either subtly or overtly, and often times are politicians or others in government or some sort of influential positions such as authors, journalists, activists, etc. To be called a kapo is to be called a traitor, but fortunately, it is not a jab at Half-Jews, while Erev Rav is on occasion, incorrectly used that way.

Personally, the Half-Jews I know are fervently pro-Israel, a far cry from any kapo or Erev Rav, and I am relieved the Law of Return added the 1970 amendment to include people like me. Though there are always groups of religious Jews who would like to change that and restrict aliyah to only those with Jewish mothers, I know that Israel is every bit my ancestral homeland as it is for people who were blessed enough to have the "right" parent be Jewish. Maybe I will never make aliyah, or maybe someday I will. At least the option is available to me, unless or until they change the law.

The Ancestry Journey Begins

When you're a Half-Jew and your Jewish heritage comes only through your father's line, ancestry and ethnicity are everything. That's why I embarked on an ancestry journey.

The Nose Knows?

The importance of the ethnic aspect of being a Jew really began during my childhood, even if I was confused about whether I was Jewish or Russian. As I stated before, my father always said that one Jew knows another and that he could tell if someone was Jewish. While that wasn't actually true because he often got it wrong (in many cases mixing up Jews and Italians), it did plant the seed in my mind that Jews have "a look." They can only have a look if they're an ethnic group.

The reality is that there is no "Jewish" appearance per se, and Jews can look quite different from one another. Skin color could be white, brown or black. The shapes of facial features can vary from rounded to sharp, from big to small, and everything in between. And there are the different Jewish ethnicities coming into play: Ashkenazi, Sephardi and Mizrahi, but also Yemeni, Ethiopian, Indian, etc. With that said, you might look at an Ashkenazi and think he must be Sephardi and vice versa. Then there are some people you would never, ever guess.

But as a child, I began searching for something tangible and realized that there are some who fall into a Mediterranean stereotype, which is what I fixated on. Italians, Greeks, Arabs and Jews can sometimes have similar features, and I admit, I searched for the stereotype. As a child, I wasn't politically correct but had an emotional need to look Jewish.

I won't call anyone out by name, but a close family member used to tell me all the time that I looked Jewish. He didn't mean it as a compliment, but I liked it anyway. And then I was informed that I had a big nose, but it was all right because I could get a nose job when I turned 18.

Well, I wasn't aware my nose was big until that time, but then I started hearing that I had a Jewish nose. Though a comment like that is usually thrown out as an insult, I began wondering whether I did have a Jewish nose. Again, this is not a politically correct topic of discussion, but these are the thoughts I had as a child.

Later on as an adult, I researched to find out, what the heck is a Jewish nose anyway? Apparently, it's really a nose common among various Mediterranean people, not specific to Jews and can also be called an aquiline (or the more derogatory, "hook") nose. Among plastic surgeons, it's far from a taboo subject, and there are websites dedicated to rhinoplasty on those with Middle Eastern or Mediterranean noses. In literature, art and pop culture, these noses have been used in a negative way to bash Jews, but also in a positive way as a source of pride for one's heritage.

Over the years, I've seen this type of nose on people from various ethnic backgrounds and know for sure it is not specific to Jews. Many Jews don't have it, and though others do, so too do non-Jews. That hook nose from the Shylock Jew depicted in anti-Semitic cartoons is a gross exaggeration, a caricature.

And my nose does not look like that, though admittedly, I do have those sort of hook nostrils, clearly visible in any profile shot (and by profile, I mean side view, rather than a social media profile picture). In any event, I decided to embrace this so-called Jewish nose because after all, negative stereotype or not, I'll take anything.

My frizzy hair was another feature I decided to embrace. It was my father who had the curly hair, not my mother, and

I held onto that. After so much analysis of my physical appearance, I determined that I inherited little from my mother's European stock. I have her eyes but otherwise look like my father or really, like his mother, my grandmother.

Even my siblings took more after our mother's side than I did. For example, I was born with dark, curly hair which then turned brown, whereas they had blonde hair which later darkened to brown. Does it mean anything? I'm not sure, but I was always the most different out of all of us, so this search for missing roots and to find where I fit in and who I resemble has always been more of an issue for me because I don't really match the rest of them. And anyway, why should I have to tiptoe around my Jewish ethnicity and carefully word it? *Well, you see, I am German and have Jewish "heritage"*—but I look more like that "heritage" I'm not allowed to discuss.

It's a funny thing to consider whether I or anyone else "looks Jewish." Many fight this idea, namely, Jews who don't necessarily have any specific look. They argue, "What does a Jew look like?" And they don't want to be left out for not looking the part when they know full well they are Jewish. Besides, converts are Jewish, and their appearance can be anything.

And then there are people who do look Jewish and are proud of it, or Half-Jews who want to prove their Jewishness, if only by the way they look. Two sides of the coin. One side screams, "How dare you stereotype Jews and say we all look a certain way!" While the other side gently asks with a skip in their voice, hands clasped together over their heart, "You think I look Jewish? Really?"

Three out of my four grandparents had blue eyes, and that includes my Jewish grandfather, giving me little chance for any other color. My Jewish grandmother, on the other hand, came from Eastern Europe but had brown eyes and a more stereotypical Middle Eastern appearance. (Stereotypical because in reality, people in the Middle East come in all shapes, sizes and colors.) In fact, on her certificate of naturalization to become an American citizen, she is described as white but with a dark complexion, purely a subjective call but interesting nonetheless. The combination of her brown eyes and my grandfather's blue eyes bore hazel eyes for my father. Some people didn't think he looked Jewish, though I did. One of the things that threw people off, aside from the last name of Miller (and most people don't realize how common the name Miller is among American Jews—they don't expect a Jew to have such a surname), was his red mustache.

They used to say that red hair originated with the Vikings, which means that anyone of Irish, Spanish or Russian descent with red hair must have some Scandinavian blood mixed in. That is not likely to be true. There have always been Jews with red hair, going all the way back to biblical times. Both Esau and King David are thought to have had red hair according to how they are described in the Tanakh, debunking the myth that Jews have red hair because they were converts somewhere along the line—Khazars or Europeans, rather than Middle Easterners.

The convert line is a favorite among anti-Semites, determined to prove Jews have no connection to Israel. They say that the Ashkenazim come from the Khazars who were converts, yet another myth debunked many times over. For one thing, there's no proof that a large Khazarian population of Iranians, Turks, Slavs and Circassians ever converted, or even a handful of Khazarian royalty, another fictitious story with no evidence to back it up.[140] [141] Secondly, the DNA testing of European Jews has proven that genetically, Jews are Jews whether they are Ashkenazi, Sephardi or Mizrahi, more related to each other than to other Europeans or Middle Easterners. So if red hair among Jews doesn't come from Europeans, it was probably there all along. But how prevalent is it?

While there aren't too many ginger Jews, there are some. In 2014, there were enough Israeli Jewish redheads to gather together for a conference. An article prompted by that conference in *The Jewish Journal* by Roger Price summarizes literary references to the red-haired Jew throughout history.[142]

He writes of two Jewish characters from British sources, Fagin from *Oliver Twist* and Shakespeare's Shylock, who was often portrayed with red hair. But then there are the "red Jews" or "di royte yidn" in Yiddish, more thoroughly explained in the article, "Redheaded Warrior Jews," by Philologos.[143] Price simply describes them as brave warriors who would come to the rescue to save their fellow Jews, a product of Yiddish folklore.

Perhaps more intriguing are the results of one study, which found that approximately 3 percent of Jews have red hair, compared to 1 percent of the general world population. This hair color occurs far more frequently among the Scottish and Irish, both over 10 percent, however it does exist among Jews and more so than in other groups. Red beards are even more common, occurring in nearly 11 percent of the Jewish males in the study.[144]

Why are these statistics important? They're not. I'm simply explaining how red hair among Jews is neither common nor uncommon but does exist. Though acquaintances of my father mistakenly believed he must have been Irish because of his red mustache, he was not some anomaly. There are redheaded Jews who are every bit as Jewish as those with black or brown hair.

Misconceptions and stereotypes regarding what a Jewish or even Middle Eastern appearance should be are widespread, especially with anti-Semites hell-bent on proving who is and isn't a Jew and why they think Jews should not be in Israel. Their logic is faulty and based on myths and lies. With that said, as a young Half-Jew looking for physical clues and evidence to prove my Jewishness to others, right or wrong, I analyzed every detail to death.

A "Jewish Gene"?

Who needs evidence to prove their Jewishness? I knew my father was Jewish, and no one had to do a DNA test or provide some certificate in order for me to know that was true. But when you're conditioned to get that "you're not a Jew" response every time you explain that it was your father who was the Jew, rather than your mother, it motivates you to show the doubters the truth. Not that anyone ever doubted my father's Jewishness, mind you. It is simply beyond my comprehension how half of my ethnic identity could be denied, especially when it's the one with which I am most connected.

And so the mission began. How do I show these people I'm Jewish? Well... science of course. Who can argue with that?

First I'd heard of a so-called "Jewish gene" and was intrigued. Much is written on the Cohens and Levis (along with all the variations of those names), whose origin can be traced biblically to the Tribe of Levi.[145] Both have more religious responsibility than other Jews, the Cohanim first, then the other Levites.[146] The Cohanim men are considered to be direct descendents of Moses' brother Aaron and members of the priesthood (as Aaron was the first High Priest of the Israelites and his sons, priests),[147] and genetic testing has demonstrated a definite distinction.[148] But there is no Cohen or Levi in my family background, and even if there were, all of this pertains to men only.

Then I read about tracking the Jewish line either matrilineally or patrilineally, i.e., the genes passed only through the female line, from mothers to daughters, or through the male line, from fathers to sons. For men, they can test the Y chromosome, and for women, it's the mito-chondrial DNA, which is passed not only from a mother to her daughters but to her sons as well. Therefore, both men and women can be tested through their mother's mitochon-drial DNA, but only men can be tested through their father's line.[149] In other words, if your mother is Jewish, your Jewish lineage can be tested, no matter if you're male or female. But if your father is Jewish, only males can be tested.

So here I am, left out in the cold. I'm a woman, and it's my father who's the Jew. It made me wonder if I was misun-derstanding something. I'm sure no scientist, and this stuff is all Greek to me. But common sense told me that if people are 50 percent of their mother and 50 percent of their father, my dad's genes were relevant. They are a part of me, and they aren't hiding.

To be honest, I had no idea what to do, so I did nothing. After all, I already knew my father was Jewish and didn't need some test to tell me, but I still hoped to connect to my Jewish side somehow.

My Father

Why not talk to my father about these issues? Easier said than done. Growing up, he rarely spoke of his family, and when he did, he would tell crazy stories, sometimes funny and sometimes melodramatic. His father was a business-man, shrewd and creative but above all, a survivor who would make things happen and wouldn't accept failure. With only a seventh grade education, he was self-taught, clever and resourceful.

One of my dad's favorite memories illustrated his father's boldness. Once, when his parents were driving down the road, they decided to stop at a little grocery store so my grandfather could run in and grab a soda. I assume my fa-ther was there judging by the way he'd tell it, and according to him, their patience was wearing thin as they waited in the car for what seemed an eternity. What was taking so long anyway? He was supposed to be in and out.

Eventually, he did come out, not as the proud owner of a new bottle of soda but of the entire store! He'd decided spontaneously to buy a small, local grocery store.

As the son of immigrants, my grandfather had that immigrant mentality: America is the land of opportunity and the only limitation to dreams is one's own hesitance. Though my dad didn't get along with his father, after his death, he would speak of him fondly, remembering his spunk.

My grandmother was a different story. Most of what my father had to say about her was negative, but one thing that stuck in my mind was that she was a big reader. As an adult, my father realized the value of reading and built up a personal library, converting a bedroom to an office with wall-to-wall bookshelves, mostly filled with nonfiction history and spy novels. This was a departure from his school days, however, when he was a terrible student and would ask his mother to read his books for him and tell him what they were about so he could pass his tests. And she would!

I'll have to keep the more colorful stories to myself, but the point is, while my father was good for sharing a little here and there about his family, he did not tell us much about his family line. Bits and pieces were all we got.

My father was fairly tight-lipped about a lot of things and quick to temper to boot, so we knew better than to ask him much. Perhaps he would have mellowed in his old age. He had already started that process, his anger transforming to depression after we'd all grown up and moved out. According to my mother, he wasn't feeling well after decades of smoking and eating all the wrong foods, his belly having grown too big for the rest of his body, creating pains in his knees.

When he was younger, he would always park at the far end of any store lot to protect his precious vehicle, but later on, he began driving around searching for the closest parking space to wherever he had to walk, placing the blame on his painful knees. In fact, he would never walk much. When my family now visits national parks or other sites where hiking is involved, we'll always partake in a few of the hikes in order to improve our experience and make the most of it, and we enjoy the walks. But when I was younger and traveled to the same sorts of places with my parents, we never did any of that. He refused to walk. We merely stopped at the scenic outlooks to take pictures.

My mother would sometimes walk around the block and would ask my father if he'd care to join her, to which he would respond, snapping, "No, I don't want to walk!" Then one day, out of the blue, he accepted, apparently realizing how out of shape he was. After about a quarter of a mile, he was so out of breath and in pain, my mother had to hurry back to the house to get the car and pick him up. He couldn't make it any further.

Shortly thereafter, chest pains sent him to the doctor. He often complained of indigestion, but this was serious enough to scare him and rightly so. The doctor told him, "I'm sending you straight to the hospital."

My dad wanted to go home first to do this and that, but the doctor said, "No way. You're not going home today."

As it turns out, he was on the verge of having a massive heart attack and needed bypass surgery, possibly a quadruple bypass. At the time, I was married and living 800 miles away. My parents described the surgery as somewhat routine nowadays, according to the doctors. They'd told him there was something like a 97 percent survival rate, and the hospital was known for its excellence in heart surgery. I think the doctors meant to calm my parents' nerves, and my parents wanted to calm mine. It worked. I didn't see the necessity of taking time off from work and getting on a plane to fly up there for that, nor did they seem to want me to do so. Instead, we talked on the phone the night before the surgery.

The conversation gave me an eerie feeling. It felt like goodbye, like he anticipated the worst.

The next day around one o'clock in the afternoon, I was struck with a sudden panic. By that time, the surgery should have been over, but my mother didn't have a cell phone back then, so all I could do was call the hospital to see how my father made out. The nurse who answered was reluctant at first, pausing before informing me in a solemn tone that my father was having a difficult time, that the entire staff was by his side, working on him. He'd made it out of surgery, but something happened.

The blood drained from my face. I knew.

All at once the need to be there emerged, and I quickly got on the phone to book a flight, rushing around to my supervisors to let them know I was leaving and had no idea when I'd be back. Fortunately, they were understanding.

By the time I got home from the office, I called the hospital again. It was too late. He was dead. My trip back would be for the funeral.

Bits and Pieces

At only 53 years-old, my father had passed away. His attitude and health would have indicated a man 20 years older, but no one could ever talk any sense into him. He was stubborn and complex to say the least. With a great sense of humor, he could make you laugh so hard you'd have tears in your eyes, but there was a dark side too. A temper. I inherited a lot of his personality, both good and bad, but I generally let things go and am far more forgiving. His anger and grudges took their toll on his heart, and it really is a shame. My relationship with him had its ups and downs, but I understood that his sensitivity was the motivating factor for his behavior. If his feelings were hurt, he would lash out in anger, rather than wallow in tears. What's funny is that I'd tell him he was sensitive, and he'd say the same about me, though he'd never accept it about himself. To him, a man had to be macho, but I think that stemmed mostly from his generation and the era when he was raised.

Not being there to see him before his death is not something I'm proud of. Do I regret it? Of course. There are many things I regret, but at the time, I was only 24 years-old and I thought he'd be fine, that there was no need to take time off from work. Besides, my father hadn't given me the impression he needed me there. Perhaps I'd misread him, but it's too late now. What's done is done, and if I could change it, I would, but I can't.

Though my relationship with my father was complicated and we'd had our arguments, when all is said and done, he was still my father. And I needed a connection to his side of the family. All I really had were some little bits and pieces that had belonged to his parents along with the tarnished Star of David my dad wore around his neck.

Over time I got all the "Jewish stuff" like the Tanakh my father got for his Bar Mitzvah. "Received upon my 13th birthday... I'm yet to be a man!" he wrote on the inside cover. It made me chuckle when I read that for the first time, imagining him at that age and what was going on in that head of his back then.

In my twenties and going through my own crises, married too young, then divorced, then remarried, then a miscarriage, and living in a foreign country, etc., I had other things on my mind and the ancestry search took a backseat to life. And by now, I couldn't ask my father about his family even if I'd wanted. The opportunity was lost.

Years went by, and things finally started to settle. There was some family drama holding me back from seriously exploring my father's line and especially from any attempt to contact anyone. Though I'd often thought about it, I couldn't, so again, I let it go.

Still, that yearning for Israel and for my people was bursting inside me. If I couldn't take a DNA test, I could at least create a family tree and get as much information out of my mother as possible. Long ago, my father had told her far more than he'd ever told his children. It was a start.

The Name

Throughout my childhood I'd always heard our family name had been some wonderfully complicated Jewish-Russian name but that when the immigrants arrived at Ellis Island, the American authorities decided it was too hard to pronounce and therefore changed it to Miller. My grandfather was born in New Jersey, but his parents had come over from Russia. The original name was lost.

Oddly enough, my grandmother had always told my father to use the name "Miller" for any documents requiring his mother's maiden name, so he was raised to believe the same thing happened to both sides of his family, the Ellis Island name change and coincidentally, Miller for both.

If my father had been Spanish and followed the culture of using two last names, that of the father first and mother second, he would have been "Miller Miller."

It was a little disappointing to be honest. Why couldn't we have an interesting ethnic name, rather than the simple and boring "Miller"? I know I'm not the only one who feels that way. There are women with beautiful Spanish or Italian last names who marry a Smith and either hyphenate or keep their maiden names not only out of pride but because they don't want to go from having a unique surname to one of the most common one-syllable names in the country. And anyway, if Miller had been our name for generations, it would have been embraced, but knowing it was forcibly changed by someone else was a different matter altogether. How could we be proud knowing the name was not adopted by choice? If Miller is your ethnic surname, that's wonderful, but that wasn't the case for us.

As children, we were told the Miller story with no further explanation until later on, when my mother revealed that my grandmother's maiden name in fact was not lost. And it wasn't Miller.

Excuse me?

That's right. It wasn't Miller, but it did start with the letter "M."

It turns out, after my grandmother passed away, my father found his parents' marriage certificates, the one in English and the one in Hebrew. For her maiden name, she did not put "Miller." She put "Mozschkovsky."[150]

If a complicated name was what I was looking for, I certainly found it! What was most striking about the name were the five consonants bunched together. Surely that spelling couldn't be correct, could it?

Misspelled or not, a smile swept over my face. Finally, I was getting somewhere, and seeing the Hebrew marriage certificate touched my heart. Of course I knew my father was Jewish and that his family had come from Russia, but here was something physical, in my hands. The document is torn and fragile and could fall apart if I'm not careful, but that makes it all the more exciting.

I still didn't know what my grandfather's family name was before Miller, but at least I knew it must have been something like Mozschkovsky, and therefore my own maiden name should be along those lines.

Beginning the Document Search

After holding onto this information for years, I finally became a paying member of the genealogical website, Ancestry.com. Money has always been tight throughout my adult life, which is what held me back from joining before. But a personal budget is all about priorities, and when I analyzed where our little bit of money went, I saw opportunity to rearrange things. It's like I always say: Some people will spend $5 on fancy coffee everyday but wouldn't dream of taking a chance on a $5 book, even if it is written about a topic that should interest them. Well, maybe I'm guilty of spending on the wrong things too. Hey, I'm only human. There was enough room in the budget for this, and after all, this is a bigger priority to me than some of the other areas draining our wallets.

The prospect of this new endeavor gave me a dopamine rush. Finally, after wondering my entire life, I could access more information than ever.

I began by starting a family tree, then proceeded to search the name of Mozschkovsky. Nothing. A Google search came up empty as well. There is nothing on that name online, although there was the possibility that it might exist spelled with the Cyrillic alphabet. Though I did take Russian in college, I remember very little, so rather than attempting to translate the name to a Russian spelling, I asked my Ukrainian Jewish friend. The response wasn't what I'd hoped.

"That spelling is impossible. Russian may be difficult, but there is no way, even in Russian, that you'd have five consonants together like that. And I've never heard that name."

Ugh.

"But aren't there variations of that name?" I asked him.

"Sure. Moskovsky, Moszkowski..." He proceeded to give me a long list of possibilities.

But inputting those names didn't help. There was nothing related to my family. Google searches on those names didn't provide much either. Back to square one.

A different approach was in order, but it was one requiring lots of time and effort. I changed my grandmother's name to Miller, one of the top 10 most common names in America. Long hours were in store for me, along with many nights going to bed with bags under my sandpaper eyes.

The effort was worth it.

Although I didn't have a lot of information on my grandmother, whom I'll call "Ruth" for the purposes of this book, I did have an idea of what year she was born and knew the exact year of her death. Also pertinent was her husband's name. I'll call him "Joseph."[151] Armed with those clues, I was able to find Ruth's listing in the Social Security Death Index and in the Philadelphia Marriage Index. Not much of a help really, considering the fact that I already had her marriage certificate in my hands and knew when she died.

Even so, just adding those sources to her name provided me with more possible documents pertaining to her. The items most likely to be connected to her are listed first in the search, but that doesn't mean it's really true. Some are, and most aren't, and then on occasion, the second page of the search is more valuable than the first. It's a question of time and clicking, reading, disregarding, and going back to the drawing board again and again.

Throughout this process, Ruth became increasingly special to me. She was with me, I'm sure, living in my heart, pushing me forward, blessing me with all the encouragement necessary to keep going. I didn't know her in life, but I'm beginning to know her now, as she is hopefully looking down, happy to see one of her son's children searching for those Jewish ties and reaching out to her through her family line. And recently, my mother came across some more trinkets that had belonged to Ruth, and she gave them to me. Among them are a couple of bracelets, which don't have much of a monetary worth but are invaluable to me as something she'd worn, once gracing her wrists as they now wrap around my own. One is made up of a series of Stars of David, while the other has her initials. I wear the tarnished pieces proudly and hope she knows when I've got them on.

Zayde

Taking a break from the Ruth search, I diverted my attention to my grandfather Joseph. So yeah. Joseph Miller. That should be easy, right?

Hardly. Imagine how common a name that is. Now as I've already indicated, Joseph was not my grandfather's name, but his real name was every bit as common. At least I had his birthday and approximate date of death, thanks to my mom and her obsession with numbers and dates. She may not remember what she had for lunch, but she will remember anything with a number, which came in handy in this ancestry search. These people were not even her family, but she cared enough to save space in her memory bank for these important dates. That German attention to facts and figures can certainly be useful at times.

Of course now I had Joseph's listing on the marriage index, and I knew his mother's name because my father's grandmother had still been alive until a few years after my parents married. My dad had talked about her fondly and obviously loved her. With a vague idea of a possible birth year, based on how old she supposedly was when she passed away, I input all the information I could, which wasn't much really.

The thing with an ancestry search is that one thing leads to another, causing a chain reaction. You may not know much about one person, but if you know something about that person's spouse, siblings, parents and grandparents, you must add whatever information you have because it all helps. Knowing Joseph's mother's name, place of birth (Russia—a vague clue but better than nothing) and year of birth give or take a few years, I could search for her. Unfortunately, she had another name that was popular back in her time, paired again with the name of Miller.

My biggest hope was to find the original name. What was it before Miller?

Little by little, I was able to fill out Joseph's family. Perhaps the most valuable public documents available are the Census reports. Thus far, they are accessible through 1940 and provide a wealth of information. For example, they list the head of the household, the children, ages, whether they're alien or naturalized and what year they arrived, where they were born, what language they spoke, where they lived, if they rented or owned and what their professions were.

There's just one small problem: not all the information was correct. Back then, Americans weren't indexed like products with barcodes as we are today, i.e. with our social security numbers, and American record-keeping wasn't exactly up to snuff. Beginning in the year 1790, the Census was taken every ten years,[152] but how did they do it? Simple. They'd send around Census-takers to walk from door-to-door, loaded with a list of questions to ask, and they'd jot down whatever answers they were given, right or wrong, often times in illegible or practically illegible handwriting.

Poring over Census records, I was shocked to learn of an unknown brother Joseph had. His name was Charles, which struck me as odd for a Jewish family back then, but it occurred to me that they may have been trying to fit in and be more American. This Charles appeared on the 1910 Census, when he was supposed to be three years-old. But on the 1920 Census, he was gone and never again appeared. My first thought was that the poor child had died, and since no one had heard of his existence, perhaps it was because Joseph was so young when his brother died that he didn't even remember him. Maybe his parents were too grief-stricken to talk about it. Maybe this and maybe that.

Years later another one of Joseph's brothers died. My father had always said he was 16 when he drowned, but the records tell a different story. I found the boy's death certificate. He was 13. Family folklore doesn't always mesh with reality. Memories fade, numbers change, and then the new memory becomes fact, even if it's wrong.

But here's the thing. If the family did talk about the teenage son who died, wouldn't they also have spoken about the toddler? I began wondering if Charles ever existed. What if it was an error on the part of the Census-taker? What if Charles belonged to the family in the next house, and he was accidentally listed on the wrong line, clumped together with the wrong family? What if, what if? We'll never know the truth.

There are many such truths that are a bit fuzzy. Joseph's family wasn't exactly focused on details, and when my grandfather's own father passed away far too early in life, Joseph was the one who provided the information for the death certificate, another document I found in my records search. First the age of 51 is written but crossed out, replaced with 47. The birth date also appears to be written in pencil and then written over in pen, and it seems to be off by a couple of years when compared to the Census data. Obviously Joseph wasn't too sure of his father's information. When he had to put the city or town where his father was born, he simply put "Russia." He didn't know the names of his father's parents and again, only put Russia for where they were born. It seems he didn't know a whole lot of anything.

This is in keeping with my father's knowledge of his family. The details had always been vague.

My grandfather Joseph's family were renters, living in a different place for each of the Census reports from 1910 to 1930. By 1940, Joseph's father had already passed away, making it that much more difficult to track his mother.

The men, I've discovered, are far easier to find than the women, who become widows and vanish. Without knowing where they went or if they remarried and later took on a new surname, it's tough to track them. They may have moved in with a daughter who married and now has a new surname. The family would be listed under the husband as the head of household, but in the case of my family, even knowing the names wouldn't help because by this time, it was already after the 1940 Census, and that's where the public access to Census records ends.

Sometimes clues come in the form of family tree sharing. One member of the site may have information on the same relative, but it's worth mentioning, the data on other family trees may not be accurate. People sometimes input information based on foggy family memories, or they may assume a person found in a search is the right one, when that may not be the case. I've had to analyze the likelihood of whether certain things are true or not.

In the case of Joseph's family, I seem to have reached a dead end. Miller is too common a name, and when I searched ship manifests from around the time Joseph's parents arrived, I never found them. Believe it or not, there are long lists of "Hebrew" Millers coming over from Russia. But how could Russian Jews have the last name of Miller?

The Miller Dilemma

The use of traditional surnames for Jews did not begin until somewhat recent times. Much like Arabs, Jews had a first name, followed by "son of" the father's name or "daughter of" the father's name. In his explanation of how Jewish surnames came about, author Bennett Muraskin uses the examples of "Moses son of Mendel (Moyshe ben Mendel)"[153] and "Feygele daughter of Moyshe (Feygele bas Moyshe)."[154] ("Bas" is the Ashkenazic version, but others use the Hebrew "bat." Think Bas Mitzvah versus Bat Mitzvah. It's the same meaning, different pronunciations.)

Though this is still a part of Jewish culture when someone gives their Hebrew name, times changed, and Jews were forced to follow the standards of their host countries for legal purposes if nothing else. When it changed depends on where in Europe they were living. Spanish Jews were the first to begin adopting surnames,[155] but the Ashkenazim held on until much later, mostly in the 18th and 19th centuries when by law, they had to either choose a surname or one would be assigned to them.[156]

The reasons for why they decided on a particular name varied. Sometimes they kept the "son of" tradition by adopting a surname with the same effect. How it turned out depended upon the language. As Muraskin wrote, in Yiddish or German, the "son of" was created by adding "son," "sohn," or "er" at the end, while in Polish or Russian it would be "wich" or "witz." The son of Mendel became Mendelsohn.[157] Other Jews took on "daughter of" in much the same way, or they adopted names with religious significance or Hebrew names. Some Jews got fancy and invented surnames by combining two German roots, often chosen from the categories of metals, adjectives, colors, flora and food, size, and words related to the heavens.[158] This is why there are so many Jews with names like Silverman, Goldstein, Fein, Weiss, Rosen, etc.

There were many who chose names for places where they lived, names which explained personal traits, or professions.[159] Professions—hmm...

Now "Miller" is a profession, but it seems unlikely someone coming from the Russian Federation would be using a name like "Miller" as opposed to a name derived from a Slavic language, possibly something ending in "sky" or "off." And yet, when I searched the ship manifests through The Statue of Liberty - Ellis Island Foundation website,[160] I found Miller after Miller arriving from Russia with the ethnicity notated as "Hebrew." (They called Jews "Hebrews" back then, and there was no political correctness, no one screaming about there not being a Jewish race.)

So how could a Russian Jew have adopted a surname like "Miller"? As I've already mentioned, according to family folklore, the name had been something else, but when the immigrants arrived at Ellis Island, the immigration authorities changed their name to Miller, something easier to pronounce and more "American." However, although that same story exists in many Jewish families, it is said to be false.[161] When I saw the ship manifests with all the Jewish Millers arriving from Russia, I realized my family very well may have adopted the surname of Miller before boarding the ship. Since I have yet to find an answer, I can only assume the intention was to sound more American. Why else would there be so many Russian-Jewish Millers?

The Census reports solidify that idea. When searching for my relatives, I came across dozens and dozens of Hebrews from Russia with the last name of Miller, many with the same first names as my ancestors, and I even found other couples with the same exact first and last names as my great-grandparents on both sides. In other words, the wife had the same first name as my great-grandmother, the husband had the same first name as my great-grandfather, their surname was Miller, they were Russian Hebrews, and their years of birth were also close. The only differences were that they lived in New York at the same time that my relatives were living in Philadelphia, and the names of their children were different. That was the only way to know they were not my relatives. And the same thing happened on the other side with the parents of my grandmother—another practically identical couple. It certainly makes the records search that much more complicated and time-consuming.

What's in a Name?

Jews had a tendency to change their first names as well. On one Census report, my great-uncle was named Isadore. On the next report 10 years later, Isadore became Issac. Another 10 years went by, and now he was Irving. Later, on his father's death certificate, he signed his name Irvin, and eventually, I discovered his nickname was Izzy. There was no question this was the same relative. He was the only son with an "I" name, and all the other information aligned correctly: age, place of birth, parents, siblings, etc. Strangely, while researching Jewish genealogy, I found an article explaining the exact same example from the author's own family search—coincidentally, a great-uncle whose name appears as Irving, Isidore and Isak.[162] When I read this, I nearly fell off my chair! Same series of names, different spellings but also for the brother of the author's grandmother. What are the odds? Or was this a common practice?

Another great-uncle of mine was Hyman, then Chaim, but eventually became Herman. The implication is clear: they were Americanizing their names.

The last name on my grandmother's side was fluid as well. Although the maiden name listed on her marriage certificate was Mozschkovsky with that complicated spelling, I never found Ruth Mozschkovsky in my document search. After finding her through the marriage index and adding all the information I could including her children's names, husband's name, etc., I eventually found her under the very name my father had always said: Miller. It turns out, he was right. Both his parents were Millers. Hebrews from Russia named Miller.

But the more I searched, the more I found. One of her brothers showed up on a document using the surname Moskovske.[163] Pretty much the same name, different spelling. I realized there was something to this name. Why were both my grandmother and great-uncle using this name if they were already Millers? I can only guess they went back to using the name their family had used back in Russia, and maybe neither really knew the correct spelling. After all, in the Cyrillic alphabet, the spelling would have been different anyway, and they were small children when they left Eastern Europe.

The same uncle used Miller later on, de-Judaizing his first name as well, but at that time while still a young man, he went with a Hebrew name combined with Moskovske. Perhaps the mindset changed, or it may have depended upon the circumstances. It seems to me, it's all about assimilation and adaptability. When Jews arrived in America, they were often escaping horrors in Europe. My family, for example, came from somewhere in the Russian Empire. The immigration authorities simply put "Russia," though some of the ship manifests used "Russian Federation," which meant "somewhere in the Russian Empire." What was Russia then is not necessarily Russia today. However, there were pogroms scattered across the land, and when I heard that the reason why my grandmother's family had left was because her house had burnt down, I knew it was likely due to a pogrom. Why else would they flee? The house burnt down, so rather than rebuild or relocate somewhere close-by, they chose to board a crowded ship with terrible living conditions to move their lives across the world to a new place they'd never seen? Surely, they were escaping.

In fact, a large wave of Jewish immigrants arrived from Russia to the United States due to Russian pogroms in the late 1800s and early 1900s. They were coming from the Pale of Settlement, where Jews were forced to live under heavy restrictions, resulting in severe poverty for many. The settlement, established in 1791 by Catherine the Great, included parts of Belorussia, Lithuania, Poland, the Ukraine and Western Russia. Life was tough for Jews confined to this place set up in part to appease Russian merchants who didn't want Jewish competition, and in part to "put Jews in their place." It was essentially a Jewish ghetto where 99 percent of the people spoke Yiddish and the children were educated in a yeshivah. This was a place where Hasidim resided, where Chabad flourished and where Jews helped each other out through charity (tzedakah).[164] [165] [166]

But it was no bed of roses. Around 40 percent of the world Jewish population resided in Pale,[167] but the hardship of living under such horrible conditions along with waves of pogroms, led many Jews to leave. Since most Jews in the

Russian Empire were forced to live in Pale and only Pale, odds are, this is where both my grandmother and grandfather's families lived and is the reason why they left. After living under oppressive conditions, the chance to start anew in the Land of Freedom, the Land of Opportunity, may have driven them to choose a so-called "American name," so they could begin again with a new identity and try to assimilate.

This is something Jews have been doing throughout history. Hadassah changed her name to Esther for the chance to marry the Persian king, leaving behind her Jewish name.[168] Sarai became Sarah when God told Abraham He would bless her and make her the mother of nations,[169] and Abram became Abraham when God made him the father of a multitude of nations.[170]

When Jews arrived in America to flee persecution and start over, they often changed their names. When they make aliyah, they return to Hebrew names. Fresh start, but this time, they are in the Jewish State where they are allowed to be Jews.

I may never know what my grandfather Joseph's family name was before Miller, but as I've learned, whatever name it had been was another adopted surname, forced upon them for legal purposes by their host nation. Aside from searching genealogy, does it matter? After all, what's in a name?

The Place

Now that things were finally starting to come together, the dream of connecting with my Jewish ancestors by filling out my family tree was becoming a reality. I was getting to know them by watching the changes in their families every ten years on the Census reports, finding death and marriage certificates, and feeling my bubbe Ruth's presence with me all the while.

One might think it should have been my father inspiring me on this journey, but he had always attempted to deter any interest in his family. If he's watching all this from up above, I have no idea if he's changed his mind, but I'd like to think my grandmother, whom I'd never met, wants me to know her family. Out of all her son's children, I'm the only one seeking her out, her death notwithstanding.

What might have happened had she lived longer? Would she have taught me how to cook matzah ball soup, potato latkes or cholent, or how to make challah? Or did she cook any of those things? I've heard stories about her opening cans for dinner, but then again, I know she could cook because my dad ranted and raved about her meatballs and loved her fried matzah so much, he got my mother to learn how to make it. We ate gefilte fish out of a jar and had lox, bagels and whitefish, but what about real cooking? I never had that grandma experience with my bubbe because she passed away two years before I was born.

By that time, my parents had already been married for five years, and my father was able to avoid his parents by using the military as an excuse, claiming to be overseas even when he wasn't. It was true he was enlisted, but the fact of the matter was, he didn't want them to know he'd married a non-Jew. But how long could that charade go on? Surely if his parents had lived longer, eventually they would have learned of his marriage and children. From what I've heard about Ruth, disappointed about the interfaith marriage or not, she would have wanted to know her grandchildren, just as I want to know her.

Then again, perhaps I built her up in my mind because I never knew her. The people in our lives tend to disappoint because they're only human after all, but the hope of some phantom grandmother being larger than life is no different from the popular icons who died too young, only to become legendary because they died in their prime. People like Marilyn Monroe or James Dean. Even President Nixon turned into a hero when he died, while in life he was viewed as a disgrace. But I think I understand Miss Ruth. I know she had her faults like anyone else, but she happened to be my grandmother, which gives her a special place in my heart, along with the only grandparent I did know, my German grandmother, also imperfect but loveable just the same.

With the theoretical encouragement of dear Ruth, I kept digging and digging into the available records. What I realized was that her family was a tad easier to find than my zayde Joseph's. While his family rented and kept moving, Ruth's family owned. That's right. They owned their home according to the Census records, despite being aliens. And they lived in the same place for a long time before moving, and after they moved, they owned the new home as well. Not only that, but her father's career remained the same all throughout, and it was unique, something rare setting these Hebrew Millers apart from all the rest: he was a harness maker.

The thing is, Hebrew Miller from Russia after Hebrew Miller from Russia, many with the same first names and born around the same time, it's a difficult task to figure out which ones are mine. But the moment I saw harness maker and kept seeing it again and again, I knew this was the lead to

110

follow. I think I need a professional genealogist to help me track down Joseph's family, but Ruth came from a more stable background, and that harness maker cleared the way.

It led to one name, then another and another, and before I knew it, I had built up quite the family tree. But there was that one loose thread nagging at me. From where in Russia did they come? Ruth had been born there, making the issue that much more critical, in my mind at least.

Pale of Settlement. Sure. That area stretched from the Baltic Sea to the Black Sea, encompassing hundreds of thousands of square miles. And one thing I learned in this journey is that the home country of immigrants from anywhere in the Russian Federation was listed simply as "Russia." But Russia today is not the same Russia as it was in the early 1900s.

My father had always told us his parents were from Russia, and any other possibility had never occurred to me. That is, until I began searching the ship manifests and came across three possibilities that might have been my relatives. Nothing lined up perfectly, as the data is sketchy at best. One document says they arrived in 1910. Another says 1913. One has them arriving together, while another has them arriving separately. Remember, the information was simply jotted down by a Census-taker who walked around visiting each house or apartment, asking questions and writing down the answers, right or wrong. Were they giving the right answers? Did they forget the exact year? Or did the Census-taker write it down wrong? Who knows?

All the name changes and unreliable dates made the search all the more difficult. Incidentally, when I looked up my German grandfather, I found all the Census reports, naturalization records, trips back and forth to Germany and re-entry to the United States, marriage and death certificates, etc., within a matter of minutes. All the information was the same on each document except for one small error of a "C" instead of a "K" in his name. Otherwise, perfect records, easy to follow and accurate.

On the other hand, my Jewish relatives had to be mysterious, leaving only clues here and there. At least there were some leads, and the search of ship manifests didn't yield any perfect results but did tip me off to one thing I'd never considered: they may not have lived in what is Russia today. It could have been Belarus, the Ukraine or somewhere else.

I had to know where. Maybe I don't have the funds to go traveling over there like they do on that ancestry show, but I simply must know the place where my grandmother lived. Armed with that information, I can read the history of that place, learn what was happening at the time they left and what happened there during the Holocaust.

The mystery deepened when my mother told me my father had always said his mother was from Bearshed, Russia. *Bearshed, like a bear's shed?* How can that be Russian? If anything, it sounds more German.

I asked my Ukrainian Jewish friend, the Israeli who's a Half-Jew on his mother's side, (making him fully Jewish though he does not discount his father's Ukrainian ethnicity). He said the same thing. It was impossible. There's no way a town in Russia would have a name like that.

Or is there?

The ancestry search is something I've been doing on and off in between writing and other projects. After a long break, one day I went back to it, and lo and behold, another member of the ancestry site had one of my great-aunts in her family tree with her town of birth listed: Bershad.

Bershad! It is located in the Ukraine. As it turns out, my Israeli friend and I are paisanos! And I am a Ukrainian Jew, at least a part of me is.

Who knows, we could even be related. Well, of course we are, 30th cousins at least. Now why he never made the leap from Bearshed to Bershad is beyond me, but at least the mystery was finally solved.

That was the good news. Finally, an answer. The bad news? Death, death and more death.

Family Ties to a Land Rich in Jewish History

In the 17th century, Bershad Jews were slaughtered in the Khmelnytsky[171] pogroms when tens of thousands of Jews were massacred by Cossacks led by Bohdan Khmelnytsky, considered a national Ukrainian hero. During this time, Ukrainian Jews were forced into martyrdom if they didn't convert, sold into slavery, gang raped, drowned, armed with weapons and forced to shoot each other, skinned alive, buried alive, chopped to pieces, butchered with knives, pierced with spears, had their limbs chopped off and their bodies thrown in the street to be trampled on by horses and wagons—basically tortured in the most horrific and evil ways imaginable.[172] [173]

There were more pogroms in the 18th century by the Haidamaks, but the Jewish community would not be killed off completely. It was a shtetl where Hasidism flourished and where tallit (prayer shawls) were produced and sold throughout the Pale of Settlement.[174] Hasidic Rebbe Raphael de Bershad, famous for his dedication to truth,[175] was based in Bershad in the 19th century. It was a place where the secular Jewish socialist labor movement, Bundism, existed as well as Zionism.[176]

In 1905, anti-Semites went on another rampage, burning down Jewish homes and businesses.[177] Ruth's family hadn't yet left for America for at least five years or as many as eight. While there don't seem to be any well-known, documented pogroms around the time Ruth's family left Bershad, her house is said to have burned down. Was it a random act of violence or a targeted anti-Semitic hate crime? Could it by chance have been an accident? If the 1905 anti-Jewish riots were the circumstances in which their house burned, they must have lived somewhere in the meantime. Even if these were not the fires prompting them to leave for good, they must have been there, experienced their shtetl burning, their friends' and families' homes and businesses destroyed, hatred and evil in the air.

With all the hardships and persecution of the Pale, whatever happened to Ruth's family house, her family escaped before more horrors, the heartbreaking devastation of the Holocaust.

According to the last Census before Ruth left Bershad, there were 7400 Jews in the town, which amounted to a little over 60 percent of the total population there.[178] After she left, civil war broke out, and yet more anti-Jewish massacres left 150 Jews dead. At least some had died fighting. Encouraged by a strong Zionist mentality, several Jews had joined forces to defend their town but lost their lives in the process.[179]

By the time World War II began, Ruth was already married to Joseph and had become a mother, but back home in Bershad, things went from bad to worse. A ghetto was established after the Germans and Romanians occupied the town, with 25,000 Jews brought in from elsewhere (Bessarabia and Bukovina).[180] The majority died from the poor living conditions, others were sent out for forced labor, and many were murdered. There were so many dead bodies, they were piling up, people frozen to death, starved to death, and the bodies of the dead who had been shot would reportedly be hung on telegraph poles for days.[181]

Some Bershad Jews fought back again. Around 50 Jews joined the underground, although the Nazis eventually killed many of them, including others falsely accused of involvement.[182]

Sadly, the Jews of Bershad fell victim to the evil impulses of the sadistic men in charge. One account tells of a Romanian commandant who enjoyed coming up with new methods to slaughter Jews. Just for kicks, he'd tie Jews to a motorcycle, dragging them down the road going as fast as he could.[183]

While it is a relief to know Ruth's family had fled long before such atrocities, there's no telling what members of the family stayed behind, which ultimately resulted in a death sentence.

Bershad, once a vibrant Jewish shtetl, was destroyed by hate. Nearly all the Jews either died or left, and though some 100 remain, this place is not what it had been before barbarians got to it. A memorial now stands dedicated to the 26,000 Jews who died in Bershad during the Holocaust, and the 200 year-old synagogue where Rebbe Raphael de Bershad once prayed continues to operate, though its roof is uneven, the old pews well-worn, prayer books crumbling apart.[184] But it survived. If its walls could talk, they might only manage to weep.

As for Joseph's parents, who left Russia before he was born, I can only assume they too lived in the Pale of Settlement since nearly all Russian Jews did. Where exactly remains a mystery, but I've no doubt their story is equally heartbreaking.

One thing is perfectly clear: these horrific acts of terror and genocide against the Jewish people are a part of my personal family history. What happened to them was not some history lesson, a vague story about strangers; these were my people. *My* people.

The Bloody Truth

As my ancestry search proceeded, I began seeing commercials on television for DNA tests. Apparently, scientists were now able to provide a basic ethnic breakdown for people sending in a DNA sample. I was intrigued. This sounded far better to me than that Y chromosome and mitochondrial DNA testing for Jews that was specific to matrilineage or patrilineage. These ethnic DNA tests were for everyone, checking one's ethnicity on both sides.

I had to do it. But how would my father's ethnicity come through? I must admit, part of me was a little panicked. What if they're right, and I'm wrong? What if there is no Jewish "race"? What if I'm Russian after all? What if the Khazar theory is right? What if my insistence all these years that I'm a Jew falls to pieces with an ethnic test result showing zero Jewish heritage?

But what if I'm right? Though that small part of me was worried, I knew deep down inside it would show the truth. My family is my blood, and Jews have blood like anyone else. If there's such a thing as Italian blood, Irish blood, German blood, etc., there has to be such a thing as Jewish blood, all political correctness aside. Jews are a people after all. The Hebrews. The Israelites. The Jews.

Then another possibility occurred to me. What if it does exist, but these scientists have not yet figured it out and therefore nothing will show up? But again, I already knew they'd done so much DNA testing over the years, enough to research Jewish diseases and to name the Jewish ethnicities of Ashkenazi, Sephardi, Mizrahi, etc. I knew they had debunked the Khazar theory and had even discovered little details like the reason why there are few alcoholics among Jews—a genetic mutation causes headaches when alcohol is consumed.[185] That's me. That information was the result of a study done all the way back in 2002. Surely by now, even these mainstream companies not focused solely on Jews can integrate all the previous Jewish research with whatever they're doing with these DNA tests. Right?

But that lingering doubt kept eating away at me. I'd always prided myself on being only two things: Jewish and German. While many of my friends growing up were all mixed up, (one of whom, as I recall, being a quarter this and an eighth that...), I was half and half.

Both of my mother's parents immigrated from Germany and were proud Germans through and through. In fact, my mother's first language was German, and she didn't speak a word of English until she was six years-old and had to go to a kindergarten where everything was taught in English. There was no ESL (English as a Second Language) back then. Foreign children were thrown into a classroom full of Americans for total immersion. Not that my mother was a foreigner; she was born in America. But with the inability to speak the native language, who could have known? The teacher couldn't understand her, and the other children would spit on her and call her a dirty German since World War II was still fresh in everyone's minds.

When I told my mom about the upcoming DNA test, she was curious and for the first time told me there was a slight possibility of finding some Czech in the results. She said that her mother's family had come from Austria and later lived on the border in Germany where there were many Czechs. And though my grandmother had light brown or dirty blonde hair, my great-grandmother had black hair. Where that came from was anyone's guess.

Still, we imagined my mother to likely be 100 percent German. But what about my father? Would he be mixed up as many suggest?

There was only one way to find out. I ordered the darn thing. It didn't take long to arrive but took far longer for me to work up the courage to actually take it. Finally, after letting it sit for a couple of weeks, I bit the bullet and did it. Now it was a waiting game.

Time ticked on, and I occupied myself with other things until the email finally arrived. There it was. The moment of truth.

You Are Who You Think You Are

With tears of joy streaming down my cheeks, I read the results. The biggest piece of the pie graph, represented in an aqua-green blotch and in unmistakable letters read, "European Jewish." Ashkenazi, in other words.

Oh my goodness. They do have the technology to prove I'm a Jew.

That's right. The biggest part of me is Jewish, far more than anything else.

The results are said to be approximations but came out as 49 percent European Jewish and 2 percent Middle Eastern. I would have to assume they are both from my father, despite not adding up to 50 percent. They are merely estimates after all.

As for the Middle Eastern bit, this could be anything including Israel, according to the DNA testing company. And knowing through other genetic studies of Ashkenazim discussed earlier in the book, combined with biblical and historical knowledge that European Jews originated in the Middle East, "European Jewish" is also Middle Eastern. That makes me around 51 percent Jewish/Middle Eastern.

And what about my supposedly 100 percent German mother?

As it turns out, my German side is a hodgepodge of various European mixed together. I'm not 50 percent German but rather, only 19 percent, if that. The results don't specify

"German" but call it "Europe West," which includes Germany and the Czech Republic (as well as France and some others). That means that if there is any Czech in there, it's mixed together with German in the ethnicity estimate.

The rest of my ethnic makeup was a huge surprise: 10 percent Scandinavian, 9 percent Italian/Greek (remember the black-haired great-grandmother?), 5 percent Eastern European (and the Czech Republic is overlapped in that section, which means that the Eastern European in me could be Czech or something else like Ukrainian), 4 percent British, less than 1 percent Spanish/Portuguese and less than 1 percent Central Asian (which includes Kazakhstan, Uzbekistan, Turkmenistan, Afghanistan, parts of Pakistan and Iran, and more).

None of these ethnicities make any sense according to my recent family history, but who knows how long ago this goes back? Scandinavian was a shock, but then the Vikings were everywhere. The Italian was a pleasant surprise since I've always had an affinity for all things Italian. I have no idea how British got mixed in, but then again, the British Empire was enormous, and like the Vikings, they were all over the place.

The point is there was no need to worry over my father's Jewish heritage being mixed. He was obviously 100 percent Jewish ethnically. It is my mother who is the mutt!

What is fascinating through all of this is Hitler and his perfect Aryan race. My mother is supposed to be completely German, but it turned out to be her side that was anything but "purebred." On the other hand, the anti-Semites are constantly rambling on about Jews being European, being Khazars or at least mixed. This is all merely a political scheme, an attempt to erase all Jewish ties to Israel. How many times must these conspiracy theories be debunked? Even I was worried what my DNA test would show with that tiny seed of doubt planted by the haters. Thankfully, the results proved what I knew all along: I am who I thought I was.

Not Exactly Half and Half

My initial reaction to the DNA results was relief, but I was also under the false impression that if we are 50 percent our fathers and 50 percent our mothers, all I had to do was double my non-Jewish ethnicities to get my mother's. Wrong.

We are not half and half exactly as our parents. While we do inherit half our DNA from our fathers and half from our mothers, it is a complex process. Out of that 50 percent, we might pull from different parts, more of one ethnicity than another, for example. It is not a genetic copy, only scaled down to 50 percent of the quantity. If it were that simple, we would be almost like a half-twin to each parent. Instead, it is a genetic recombination. Though we may be half each parent genealogically, genetically one ethnicity may come through more dominantly than another.[186] [187]

Think about it. If that wasn't the case, all siblings would come out like twins, without having to be born together. While all children get 50 percent of their DNA from each parents, it comes out in varied combinations.[188] One sibling might show up as being 15 percent British while another could be 5 percent. Still another might be 35 percent. It all has to do with the genetic recombination. Some blondes have brunette or ginger siblings, and one child might be light-skinned while another has far darker skin. How did they turn out so differently?

If one ethnicity comes through more than another, it means that we cannot make assumptions or try to guess the ethnic genetic makeup of our siblings or even our parents—unless, that is, our parents truly are 100 percent of one thing. It would certainly seem that way when it comes to my father, but he is no longer around to test. However, my mother is, and she did decide to take her own DNA test.

The results shocked me yet again. Though I am only 19 percent German and had wrongly assumed she would be 38 percent (because I'd merely doubled my own percentage), her genetic makeup was far different than expected. As it turns out, my mother is 70 percent German. It's a far cry from 100 percent, but it's certainly more than 38.

Let's compare my ethnicities to my mother's:

She is 70 percent German; I am 19.

She is 12 percent British; I am 4.

She is 4 percent Eastern European; I am 5.

She is 4 percent Spanish/Portuguese; I am less than 1.

She is 3 percent Italian/Greek; I am 9.

She is 2 percent Scandinavian; I am 10.

She is 1 percent Middle Eastern; I am 2 but figured it was from my father, though I might be wrong. She also happens to be 2 percent European Jewish! I am 49 percent, but of course this comes from my father. And finally, my mother has two ethnicities that she didn't share with me: She is 1 percent Finnish/Northwestern Russian and less than 1 percent Southern Asian, which is the Indian Subcontinent. (Who knew?)

Another interesting fact is that so far, there are only 37 DNA matches to my mother on the Ancestry website. These matches are other customers who have also taken the DNA test and are showing up as being related somehow. In her case, they are cousins, mostly distant.

My husband also took the DNA test and turned out to be 5 percent European Jewish, something we'd never known. The rest is quite a mixture. He too has few matches, only 43 so far. (I say "so far" because as more customers take the test, more relatives could show up.)

And yet as of now, I have nearly 800 matches on the site, mostly through my Jewish side. Yes, we are all related!

Living Relatives

When my father cut himself off from his family, he took on a possessive attitude, behaving as if these people belonged to him and him alone. What he failed to realize was that once he had children of his own, he now shared his relatives with his offspring, and it wasn't right to isolate us.

Who were these relatives, and what would it have been like had they been a part of our lives? Contacting them had been discouraged, but nearly 18 years after my father's death, I finally decided to make an attempt. I'd steer clear of the family drama and focus on Ruth's side. After all, one name kept calling me like a magnet.

Throughout my ancestry search, Ruth's harness maker father and youngest brother were the key to everything. That brother was the only one born in the United States, and he stayed close to his father. On the last public Census report of 1940, Ruth's baby brother was already married and had one child, and the three were living with Ruth's parents. When their father died, it was that brother who had signed the death certificate, and his son was my father's first cousin. Still a young child on the 1940 Census, he was the only one from my father's generation I could find in the records. For the purposes of this book, I'll call him Morty.[189]

I wondered if Morty was still alive. The likelihood was high, although my own father was only 53 when he passed away. We never know when our time will come, but I had to be optimistic.

On the genealogical site, it's been easier for me to find data on grandparents and great-grandparents than younger relatives. This is mostly due to the fact that the Census reports stop after 1940, and the women disappear once they marry or become widows. Without knowing their married names or where they went, it's an uphill climb. And without knowing what happened to the women, much is lost. On the 1940 Census, I'd only found one cousin of my father's. Most of the rest either hadn't been born yet or weren't as easy to find without the help of an expert.

Then one day I received a message on the genealogical website from someone telling me that we're related. She said that Sara Friedman[190] was her great-aunt. As it turned out, Sara was married to my great-uncle, and this lady was wrong about us being related, though we do share an obvious connection. With that said, it was a breakthrough. Sara Friedman was Morty's mother! She was married to the harness maker's son, my grandmother's baby brother.

We began messaging back and forth, and one thing led to another. This lady suggested I take a look at some online obituaries, which were a great help, but most importantly, she provided me with the website of the company Morty's father had started. This company spanned the generations from Ruth's brother, who founded it, to his son Morty, Morty's sons and now a grandson as well. Bingo!

The obituaries provided me with more names I'd never seen before, my father's cousins and their children, who are my second cousins. From there I went to social media and found Morty! I sent friend requests to a few of my second cousins, along with messages, but most of them deleted my requests because they had no idea who I was. One did respond, and we had a nice conversation. She even mentioned Morty.

The friend request to Morty went unanswered, and I realized I'd never get anywhere this way because there are so many Millers in the world, it would be impossible for them to know me. But I had another trick up my sleeve—the company website.

Quickly finding the "contact us" section of the site, I sent an email that probably sounded a little crazy. Though I don't remember exactly what I wrote, it was something about who my father was and how I'd been doing an ancestry search and believe Morty is my father's first cousin.

The next day I received an email from Morty, asking me to call him. And that was that!

Dear Morty is the loveliest man. Of course he knew my father and shared many stories, while I did the same, catching him up to speed on whatever happened to his long lost cousin. Although we have yet to meet in person, we have spoken on the phone a few times, and he's sent me some invaluable photographs of my grandparents (including two from their wedding day), of my great-grandparents, and a group photo of the entire family from the wedding of one of the cousins. He also told me another cousin wanted to speak to me, and now I've called her as well and have messaged with a few more relatives. Unfortunately they all live far away, but the communication lines are open.

Most of my second cousins have no interest, but I really couldn't expect any different. They didn't know my father, so why should they care about me? My father's first cousins are another story. They knew my dad, and I am an extension of him. Furthermore, most of the cousins were close, so close in fact that many of the second cousins, i.e. my generation, were raised as if they were first cousins. With that kind of warmth in the family, it truly is mystifying why my siblings and I were robbed of that growing up.

The good news is that now I have a connection to my father's side of the family and am gradually getting to know Morty's daughter. Hopefully, the interest in me will not wane when the novelty of a new relative no longer excites, and one day I will meet my father's sweet cousin Morty, along with the rest. Most importantly, my Jewish heritage lives on.

Should a Half-Jew Convert?

I am a Jew. Such a simple statement, yet one so few can make. If I converted in an Orthodox synagogue, I could say those words without second-guessing and without the standard spiel of: well you see... my father... and I identify as... I feel closer to...

Just a simple, "I am a Jew," and that's that.

But—

I already am a Jew. Halakhah or not, no one can deny my Jewishness on the ethnic level. And the problem with converting is, to some, a convert will always be a convert with a distinction between them and ethnic Jews. That is not how it is supposed to be, and there are those who agree that once someone converts to Judaism, there is no difference. However, there are others who will never see converts in the same way. If I were to convert, my ethnicity would no longer be relevant because at the mere mention of the word "convert," that is all some will hear. Is it right? Is this how it should be? No, of course not, but I have to be realistic.

Harry[191] is a Jewish friend of mine. Years ago, he married a third generation Greek-American, whose family was Christian. Their interfaith marriage must have been a little tricky, but Harry and his wife raised their three boys in the mother's congregational church, also attending temple several times. As they got older, two of their sons met with Harry's rabbi to see about converting to Judaism. Once the rabbi told them a Reform conversion would not be recognized in Israel, they decided not to bother. This is the reality of converting. If they'd wanted to go through an Orthodox conversion, that would be recognized, however they would be in the same boat as me: forever viewed as converts.

Now there is a provision in Judaism for non-Jews known as Noahidism with seven laws. Noahides need only worry about following these important Seven Laws of Noah, rather than the 613 Jewish mitzvot or commandments. These seven laws[192] are easy to follow (for me at least):

Do not deny God.

Do not blaspheme God.

Do not murder.

Do not engage in sexual immorality.

Do not steal.

Do not eat of a live animal.

Establish courts/legal system.

There is a little more complexity to the laws, which are explained in greater detail at Chabad.org.[193]

I could simply live my life as a Noahide, and perhaps I will. What I do know is that I am an ethnic Jew, no matter what religious laws say or don't say. For now, I don't plan to convert to be what I already am. There will always be some who call me a Gentile or even a goy, and there will be others who accept me as a Jew. Either way, my life as a Half-Jew may be halfway confusing, but then life is never easy anyway. Like most people, I will forever live within those shades of grey.

Jew or Gentile, I am what I am.

Afterword

Thank you for reading this book. If you can identify with the difficulties of growing up interfaith or are currently in an interfaith marriage and worry about how to raise your children, I hope this book provided the insight you need. Or if you started the book with a strong belief contrary to my own views, determined to prove me wrong, I do hope this book has, if nothing more, opened your mind to a better understanding.

There are many Half-Jews like me. People who love Israel with every fiber of their being, and who love the Jewish people, who consider Jews as their people. We don't want to be dismissed or insulted.

Is there a solution to this issue? I don't know the answer. All I can do is give a little perspective.

In my novel, *The Religion of the Heart*, as Catherine discovers her identity is not quite what she thought it was, she is frazzled. Abdul attempts to calm her nerves by telling her, "You're just Catherine. Forget the rest."

I purposely use practically the same line again in *Secrets of the Heart* for a similar circumstance of confused identity. This is the only advice I can really give to Half-Jews or anyone else who doesn't quite fit the mold. You are you. That's who you are and all you ever need to be.

If you have enjoyed this book, please leave me a review on Amazon.com, Goodreads or other review sites, and spread the word to friends and family. Thank you for taking the time to read my work.

I'd also like to thank those who gave me permission to use their answers to my questions in this book. Your input is greatly appreciated.

Other Books by D.M. Miller

The Religion of the Heart
(Heart Series, Volume 1)

Catherine and Abdul come from two opposing worlds. She is raised in the Judeo-Christian West, while he comes from a Muslim family in Egypt. Their first meeting is little more than a fleeting moment, but it sparks over a decade-long desperation and agonizing battle to be together.

Incompatible religions, distinct cultures and hot-tempered families vowing to keep them apart are the overwhelming hurdles they face, and reality hits once mysteries are solved and the fairytale beginning fades away. They are left with difficult decisions as they determine how important their respective religions are and whether or not the Muslim culture can mesh with the West.

Can an enduring yet taboo love conquer all when conflicting religions are duking it out, or will threatening roadblocks stand in the way?

Agony of the Heart
(Heart Series, Volume 2)

Does he still love her? That's what Catherine wants to know, her desperate longing unanswered, as life and prior dreams fall flat. Fervently searching for what was and what should be, her downward spiral leaves Abdul scratching his head. Picking up the shattered pieces is not easy, and the man who turned his life upside down has crucial choices to make.

Throw a Muslim, a Jew, determination, disappointment, anti-Semitism and claims of Islamophobia in a pot, and the result is a steamy stew of emotional turmoil. Yet what it boils down to is one all-consuming basic need.

With shocking cultural differences, relatives foaming at the mouth and goals on opposing trajectories, the fight to keep it together is looming large. Is their love strong enough to withstand it all? And will they triumph against the formidable mountains standing in their way?

Secrets of the Heart
(Heart Series, Volume 3)

Life is full of surprises, but no one is more surprised than Catherine when a mysterious figure from her past arrives uninvited. Suddenly, deception and lies rear their ugly head when everything she thought she knew turns upside down.

Abdul's challenges intensify, and his respect for his wife is questioned by someone new occupying her heart. Hostility and jealousy dominate while battles unfold, and the contrasting journeys of two people merge.

Religion, ethnicity, culture, nationality and above all, family, are intertwined in the search for truth when secrets slowly reveal a shocking reality. Previous perceptions transform, creating fresh loyalties...

With Catherine's beginnings coming to light, the struggle between ancestral DNA and adopted love emerges. Is blood really thicker than water? And how is identity truly defined?

Dandelion Fuzz
(Poetry Collection)

Deep within the most guarded sections of the soul is a heart-ache, desperately begging for release. These poems provide that catharsis, that cleansing, essential for the greater happiness waiting around the corner with a welcoming embrace. Wring the tears out of the heart and start anew: take a dandelion, blow away the fuzz and make a wish.

More novels from the Heart Series are coming soon!

Stay up-to-date by following D.M. Miller on:

Amazon
https://www.amazon.com/D.M.-Miller/e/B012RDNV76/

Wordpress Blog https://dmmillerauthor.wordpress.com

Facebook
https://www.facebook.com/dmmillerauthor/

Endnotes

[1] In Genesis 12: 1-3, God tells Abram He will make of him a great nation, that He will bless him, make his name great, bless those who bless Abram and curse those who curse him.

[2] This is based on the 2016 world population estimated at around 7.4 billion people, along with the assumption that a 2015 report issued by the Jewish People Policy Institute (JPPI) and reported by ynetnews.com (http://www.ynetnews.com/articles/0,7340,L-4673018,00.html) that the world Jewish population in 2015 stood at nearly 16 million, is correct.

[3] Vital Statistics: Jewish Population of the World, Data compiled by The Jewish Virtual Library from the following sources: Sergio DellaPergola. "World Jewish Population, 2012." The American Jewish Year Book (2012) (2014) (Dordrecht: Springer) p. 212-283. Population Reference Bureau. Link: http://www.jewishvirtuallibrary.org/jsource/Judaism/jewpop.html

4 Kravitz, Derek. "New York City Area's Jewish Population Rises." *The Wall Street Journal*, 1 October 2013. http://www.wsj.com/articles/SB10001424052702304373104579109671933282670

[5] Ibid.

[6] Berkenwald, Leah. "What Is Jewish Hair?" *Jewish Women's Archive, Blog: Jewesses with Attitude,* 26 October 2009. http://jwa.org/blog/jewish-hair

[7] "What Is a 'Jewish Name'?" *Avotaynu.* http://www.avotaynu.com/csi/jewishname.htm Avotaynu is a Jewish genealogy website, which states that the third most common Jewish surname in the United States after Cohen and Levy is Miller.

[8] Rabbi Sacks. "Why I Am a Jew." *Youtube*, 9 September 2015. https://www.youtube.com/watch?v=CAbiFbpQP8o (Produced by whiteanimation.com/silueta.co.il for The Office of Rabbi Sacks, www.rabbisacks.org.)

[9] Name has been changed to protect the privacy of the individual mentioned.

[10] Kolatch, Alfred J. (1981). *The Jewish Book of Why* (p 14). Middle Village, NY: Jonathan David Publishers, Inc.

[11] Ibid.

[12] Genesis 5:4-32

[13] There are too many examples of this to list, but here are but a few: Exodus 6:8, Genesis 12:7, Genesis 26:2-5, Genesis 13:15, Genesis 15:7, Genesis 15:18, Genesis 17:8, Genesis 50:24, Deuteronomy 6:10, Deuteronomy 31:20, Joshua 5:6, Judges 2:1, etc.

[14] Genesis 17:20

---

[15] Genesis 17: 19, 21

[16] Genesis 17: 16

[17] Housman, Mordechai. "A Little Bit About Me." *beingjewish.com.* http://www.beingjewish.com/misc/aboutme.html Housman describes himself as Hassidic, "a fifth-generation Karlin-Stolin Chosid by patrilineal descent" (notice "patrilineal descent"), whose education includes several Yeshivahs, as well as a Bachelor's degree in journalism and Judaic Studies. Although not an ordained rabbi, Housman has experience teaching Judaism to newcomers.

[18] Housman, Mordechai. "Who Is a Jew, According to the Torah?" *beingjewish.com.* http://www.beingjewish.com/identity/whoisajew.html

[19] A clear and concise list can be found here: Rich, Tracey R. "A List of the 613 Mitzvot (Commandments)", *Judaism 101.* http://www.jewfaq.org/613.htm

[20] Deuteronomy 7:1-2.

[21] Deuteronomy 7:3

[22] Deuteronomy 7:4

[23] (1985) *Tanakh, A New Translation of The Holy Scriptures According to the Original Hebrew Text.* Philadelphia, Jerusalem: The Jewish Publication Society

[24] Chabad.org: The Complete Jewish Bible with Rashi Commentary.

[25] Deuteronomy 7:5

[26] Read Esther's story in The Book of Esther. She was the Jewish Hadassah who married the Persian King Ahasuerus, thought to be King Xerxes I.

[27] The Book of Esther 2:7

[28] Ezra 6:15

[29] Ezra 9:1

[30] Ezra 9:2

[31] Ezra 10: 10-11

[32] "Ethnic Jewish Groups Summary." *The Incredible Story of the Jewish People.* http://www.the-jewish-story.org/ethnic.html

[33] Wade, Nicholas. "Y Chromosome Bears Witness to Story of the Jewish Diaspora." *The New York Times*, 9 May 2000. http://www.nytimes.com/2000/05/09/science/y-chromosome-bears-witness-to-story-of-the-jewish-diaspora.html

[34] "European Jewish Ethnicity." *dna.ancestry.com.* http://dna.ancestry.com/ethnicity/european-jewish

[35] Rich, Tracey R. "Ashkenazic and Sephardic Jews." *Judaism 101.* http://www.jewfaq.org/ashkseph.htm

[36] Solomin, Rabbi Rachel M. "Sephardic, Ashkenazic, Mizrahi and Ethiopian Jews." *My Jewish Learning.* http://www.myjewishlearning.com/article/sephardic-ashkenazic-mizrahi-jews-jewish-ethnic-diversity/

[37] "Ethiopia." *Jewish Virtual Library.*
http://www.jewishvirtuallibrary.org/jsource/Judaism/ejhist.html
38 There are many short articles to read for a brief overview of each rescue mission to Ethiopia. The IDF Blog is one place to start and is a reliable source as it was the IDF, Israeli Defense Forces, which carried out the missions. Here are a few: "1984-1991 Airlift of Ethiopian Jewish community." *idfblog.com*, 3 August 2013. https://www.idfblog.com/about-the-idf/history-of-the-idf/1984-1991-airlift-of-ethiopian-jewish-community/; "Today in History: IDF Airlifts 14,500 Ethiopian Jews to Israel." *idfblog.com*, 25 May 2014.
https://www.idfblog.com/blog/2014/05/25/today-history-idf-airlifts-14500-ethiopian-jews-israel/; "Journeys to Freedom: IDF Rescue Operations." *idfblog.com*, 25 April 2016. https://www.idfblog.com/blog/2016/04/25/journeys-freedom-idf-rescue-operations/
[39] "People Are Not as Alike as Scientists Once Thought." *The Tech, Museum of Innovation, Stanford at the Tech, Understanding Genetics.*
http://genetics.thetech.org/original_news/news38
[40] Ritter, Malcolm, *Associated Press.* "Study: Humans' DNA Not Quite So Similar." *USA Today*, 4 September 2007.
http://usatoday30.usatoday.com/news/health/2007-09-03-dna-differences_N.htm
[41] New York University Medical Center And School Of Medicine. "Jews Are The Genetic Brothers Of Palestinians, Syrians, And Lebanese." *Science Daily*, 9 May 2000. <www.sciencedaily.com/releases/2000/05/000509003653.htm>.
[42] Butnick, Stephanie. "Study Says All Ashkenazi Jews are 30th Cousins." *Tablet Magazine*, 10 September 2014.
http://www.tabletmag.com/scroll/184252/study-says-all-ashkenazi-jews-are-30th-cousins
[43] Associated Press. "Many Ashkenazi Jews Descended from 4 Women." *YnetNews.com*, 13 January 2006. http://www.ynetnews.com/articles/0,7340,L-3199788,00.html
[44] Ibid.
[45] Ibid.
[46] Roach, John. "8 Jewish Archaeological Discoveries." *NBC News.*
http://www.nbcnews.com/id/28162671/ns/technology_and_science-science/t/jewish-archaeological-discoveries/#.WB1bmPkrKM8
[47] ADL. "Blood Libel: A false, incendiary claim against Jews." *Anti-Defamation League (ADL).* http://www.adl.org/anti-semitism/united-states/c/what-is-the-blood-libel.html?referrer=https://www.google.com/#.WBpyofkrKM8

[48] "Encyclopedia Judaica: Blood Libel." *Jewish Virtual Library*, 2008. http://www.jewishvirtuallibrary.org/jsource/judaica/ejud_0002_0003_0_03147. html

49 Khalaji, Mehdi. "The Classic Blood Libel Against Jews Goes Mainstream in Iran." *The Washington Institute*, 21 April 2015. http://www.washingtoninstitute.org/policy-analysis/view/the-classic-blood-libel-against-jews-goes-mainstream-in-iran

[50] Fiske, Gavriel. "Egyptian Politician Revives Classic Passover Blood Libel." *The Times of Israel,* 19 June 2013. http://www.timesofisrael.com/egyptian-politician-revives-passover-blood-libel/

[51] Pontz, Zach. "Egyptian Newspaper Features Two Blood Libel Articles in a Single Day." *The Algemeiner*, 1 May 2013. https://www.algemeiner.com/2013/05/01/egyptian-newspaper-features-two-blood-libel-articles-in-a-single-day/

[52] Sussman, Robert Wald. "There Is No Such Thing as Race." *Newsweek*, 8 November 2014. http://www.newsweek.com/there-no-such-thing-race-283123

[53] "What Is the Impact of Genetics on Health and Disease?" *The American Society of Human Genetics (ASHG)*. http://www.ashg.org/education/medical_genetics.shtml

[54] Ibid.

[55] Ibid.

[56] Jaslow, Ryan. "BRCA Test Leads Angelina Jolie to Get Double Mastectomy: Who Should Get Tested?" *CBS News*, 14 May 2013. http://www.cbsnews.com/news/brca-test-leads-angelina-jolie-to-get-double-mastectomy-who-should-get-tested/

[57] Weintraub, Arlene. "Angelina Jolie Sparks Rise in Genetic Testing for Treat Breast Cancer." *Cure Today*, 19 October 2015. http://www.curetoday.com/publications/cure/2015/breast-2015/the-jolie-effect

[58] Jaslow, Ryan. "BRCA Test Leads Angelina Jolie to Get Double Mastectomy: Who Should Get Tested?" *CBS News*, 14 May 2013. http://www.cbsnews.com/news/brca-test-leads-angelina-jolie-to-get-double-mastectomy-who-should-get-tested/

[59] Rabin, Roni Caryn. "Study of Jewish Women Shows Link to Cancer Without Family History." *The New York Times*, 4 September 2014. http://www.nytimes.com/2014/09/05/health/05cancer.html?_r=0

[60] Weintraub, Arlene. "Angelina Jolie Sparks Rise in Genetic Testing for Treat Breast Cancer." *Cure Today*, 19 October 2015.

[61] "Jewish Genetic Diseases." Jewish Genetic Disease Consortium (JGDC). http://www.jewishgeneticdiseases.org/jewish-genetic-diseases/

[62] "Tay-Sachs Disease." Jewish Genetic Disease Consortium (JGDC). http://www.jewishgeneticdiseases.org/diseases/tay-sachs-disease/

[63] "Jewish Genetic Diseases." Jewish Genetic Disease Consortium (JGDC). http://www.jewishgeneticdiseases.org/jewish-genetic-diseases/
[64] Ibid.
[65] "Genetic Diseases." Genetic Disease Foundation. http://www.geneticdiseasefoundation.org/genetic-diseases/
[66] "Race and Ethnicity: Clues to Your Heart Disease Risk?" *Harvard Health Publications, Harvard Medical School*, August 2015. http://www.health.harvard.edu/heart-health/race-and-ethnicity-clues-to-your-heart-disease-risk
[67] "The 'Uniqueness' of Ashkenazi Jewish Ancestry Is Important for Health." *23andMe Blog*, 22 May 2012. https://blog.23andme.com/ancestry/the-uniqueness-of-ashkenazi-jewish-ancestry-is-important-for-health/
[68] *Who Do You Think You Are?* Season 4, Episode 3, Release Date 6 August 2013. "Media mogul Chelsea Handler confronts a deep family secret: her Grandfather's rumored Nazi past. As she dives into her family's struggle to survive in a desperate time, the details uncovered will finally confirm or deny his affiliation to the dark regime."
[69] Mizoguchi, Karen. " 'Don't Ever Say I'm Not a Real Jew!' Chelsea Handler Sports Big Hair at Her Bar Mitzvah in Eighties Throwback Shot." *Daily Mail*, 1 August 2014. http://www.dailymail.co.uk/tvshowbiz/article-2713799/Chelsea-Handler-sports-big-hair-bar-mitzvah-Eighties-throwback-shot.html (Should be "Bat Mitzvah" rather than "Bar Mitzvah," but that was the actual title of the article.)
[70] Kim, Eddie. "Tough Talking Chelsea Handler Breaks Down As She Discovers Grandfather's Nazi Past in New Episode of Who Do You Think You Are?" *Daily Mail*, 7 August 2013. http://www.dailymail.co.uk/tvshowbiz/article-2385798/Tough-talking-Chelsea-Handler-breaks-discovers-grandfathers-Nazi-past-new-episode-Who-Do-You-Think-You-Are.html
[71] Press Release. "The Big Lie of Israeli 'Organ Harvesting' Resurfaces As YouTube Video on Haiti Earthquake Goes Global." *Anti-Defamation League (ADL)*, 21 January 2010. http://www.adl.org/press-center/press-releases/miscellaneous/the-big-lie-of-israeli-organ.html?referrer=https://www.google.com/#.WB-cjPkrKM8
[72] Bender, Dave. "TIME Magazine Retracts IDF Organ Theft Claim Following Criticism (Update)." *The Algemeiner*, 14 August 2014. https://www.algemeiner.com/2014/08/24/time-magazine-slammed-for-resurrecting-unsubstantiated-idf-organ-theft-blood-libel-video/
[73] Ziri, Danielle. "Danon Asks UN to Condemn Organ-Harvesting 'Blood Libel.' " *The Jerusalem Post*, 5 November 2015. http://www.jpost.com/Arab-Israeli-Conflict/Israel-blasts-Palestinians-after-accusations-of-organ-harvesting-432085
[74] McNeil Jr., Donald G. "Finding a Scapegoat When Epidemics Strike." *The New York Times*, 31 August 2009. http://www.nytimes.com/2009/09/01/health/01plague.html

[75] Saltzman, Sammy. "Jews Responsible for All 'Wars in the World,' But Mel Gibson Not Responsible for DUI Anymore." *CBS News*, 7 October 2009. http://www.cbsnews.com/news/jews-responsible-for-all-wars-in-the-world-but-mel-gibson-not-responsible-for-dui-anymore/ (Gibson's tirade is simply one example, but this is an anti-Semitic canard repeated often and around the world.)

[76] Bergman, Ronen. "Abbas' Book Reveals: The 'Nazi-Zionist Plot' of the Holocaust." *Ynet News*, 26 November 2014. http://www.ynetnews.com/articles/0,7340,L-4596121,00.html

[77] Foxman, Abraham H. "Blaming the Jews: The Financial Crisis and Anti-Semitism." *Anti-Defamation League (ADL)*, 13 November 2008. http://archive.adl.org/main_anti_semitism_international/blaming_jews_financial.html#.WB-K5_krKM8

[78] Dershowitz, Alan. "Do Jews Control the Media?" *The Huffington Post,* 25 May 2011. http://www.huffingtonpost.com/alan-dershowitz/do-jews-control-the-media_b_753227.html

[79] Foxman, Abraham H. (2003.) *Never Again? The Threat of the New Anti-Semitism.* (pp. 248-251). HarperSanFrancisco, A Division of HarperCollins Publishers.

[80] Elder of Ziyon. "Cleric Accuses Israel of Using Jinn Demons to Spy on Iran (Update)." *Elder of Ziyon*, 29 June 2014. http://elderofziyon.blogspot.com/2014/06/cleric-accuses-israel-of-using-jinn.html (Note: Elder of Ziyon may be a blogger, but his column has been reproduced in highly respected Israeli newspapers. He always uses real references to back up his articles, and he explains, in case you don't realize, his name is meant to be ironic.)

[81] Associated Press. "Stork Busted As Suspected Spy in Egypt." *New York Daily News*, 31 August 2013. http://www.nydailynews.com/news/world/stork-busted-cairo-spy-flap-article-1.1442728

[82] Reuters. "Bird Accused of Spying for Israel Released by Turkish Authorities." *New York Daily News*, 26 July 2013. http://www.nydailynews.com/news/world/turkey-frees-bird-accused-spying-article-1.1409894

[83] Daily Mail Reporter. "Vulture Tagged by Israeli Scientists Flies into Saudi Arabia... and Is Arrested for Being a Spy." *Daily Mail*, 5 January 2011. http://www.dailymail.co.uk/news/article-1344019/Vulture-tagged-Israeli-scientists-flies-Saudi-Arabia-arrested-spy.html

[84] Bennett-Smith, Meredith. "Vulture 'Spying for Israel' Caught in Sudan As Rumors Swirl About Feathery Secret Agents." *The World Post, A Partnership of The Huffington Post and Berggruen Institute*, 11 December 2012. http://www.huffingtonpost.com/2012/12/11/vulture-spying-for-israel-caught-sudan-secret-agents-sudan_n_2278512.html

[85] Ronen, Gil. "Egyptian Official Blames Mossad for Sinai Shark Attacks." *Arutz Sheva 7, Israel National News*, 6 December 2010. http://www.israelnationalnews.com/News/News.aspx/141021#.UnAZ7CTn-M-

[86] Abu Toameh, Khaled and Keinon, Herb. "Report: Abbas Accuses Israel of Using Wild Boars Against Palestinians." *The Jerusalem Post*, 22 November 2014. http://www.jpost.com/Arab-Israeli-Conflict/PA-chief-warns-against-resorting-to-religious-war-382499

[87] Abu Toameh, Khaled. "Hamas Naval Commandos Arrest Dolphin Who 'Spied for Israel.' " *The Jerusalem Post*, 19 August 2015. http://www.jpost.com/Arab-Israeli-Conflict/Hamas-naval-commandos-arrest-dolphin-who-spied-for-Israel-412579

[88] Official Blogs from the Anti-Defamation League. "Allegations that Israel Is Behind ISIS Emerge on Al Jazeera." *Anti-Defamation League (ADL)*, 24 August 2015. http://blog.adl.org/international/allegations-that-israel-is-behind-isis-emerge-on-al-jazeera

[89] "Anti-Semitic 9/11 Conspiracy Theorists Thrive 15 Years After Attacks." *Anti-Defamation League (ADL)*, 9 September 2016. http://blog.adl.org/anti-semitism/anti-semitic-911-conspiracy-theorists-thrive-15-years-after-attacks

[90] "Cartoon Collection." *Palestinian Media Watch (PMW)*. http://palwatch.org/site/modules/cartoons/cartoons.aspx

[91] "Palestinian Videos." *Palestinian Media Watch (PMW)*. http://palwatch.org/SITE/MODULES/videos/pal/videos.aspx

[92] Benari, Elad. "Netanyahu: Time for Abbas to Stop Celebrating with Terrorists." *Arutz Sheva 7, Israel National News*, 3 January 2014. http://www.israelnationalnews.com/News/News.aspx/175864

[93] The Tower.org Staff. "Fatah, Abbas Celebrate 50 Years of Terror by Glorifying Violence, Denying Israel." *The Tower*, 2 January 2015. http://www.thetower.org/1478-fatah-abbas-celebrate-50-years-of-terror-by-glorifying-violence-denying-israel/

[94] Times of Israel Staff. "Abbas Confirms PA Still Paying Terrorists' Salaries- Report." *The Times of Israel*, 7 May 2016. http://www.timesofisrael.com/abbas-confirms-pa-still-paying-terrorists-salaries-report/

[95] Reuters. "Palestinians in Gaza Celebrate Terror Attack at Jerusalem Synagogue." *The Jerusalem Post*, 18 November 2014. http://www.jpost.com/Arab-Israeli-Conflict/Palestinians-in-Gaza-celebrate-deadly-Jerusalem-synagogue-attack-382125

[96] "Schoolbooks." *Palestinian Media Watch (PMW)*. http://palwatch.org/main.aspx?fi=122

[97] Fendel, Hillel. "Report: Abbas' Holocaust-Denial Dissertation Widely Taught in PA." *Arutz Sheva 7, Israel National News*, 28 April 2011. http://www.israelnationalnews.com/News/News.aspx/143752

[98] Tuttle, Ian. "The Media's Shameful, Shameless Bias Against Israel." *National Review,* 15 October 2015. http://www.nationalreview.com/article/425651/medias-shameful-naked-bias-against-israel-ian-tuttle

[99] Aharoni, Ido. "How the United Nations Human Rights Council Unfairly Targets Israel." *Time,* 30 July 2014. http://time.com/3060203/united-nations-human-rights-council-israel/

[100] Emerson, Steven. "The International Media Bias Against Israel Is Beyond the Pale." *The Algemeiner,* 3 April 2016. https://www.algemeiner.com/2016/04/03/the-international-media-bias-against-israel-is-beyond-the-pale/

[101] *WTF* with Marc Maron, Episode 623, 27 July 2015. http://www.wtfpod.com/podcast/episodes/episode_623_-_jason_segel

[102] Tobin, Andrew. "Jason Segel Opens Up to Marc Maron About Childhood As Jewish Outsider." *Haaretz,* 31 July 2015. http://www.haaretz.com/beta/1.668844?utm_campaign=Echobox&utm_medium=Social&utm_source=Facebook

[103] Ibid.

[104] "Jewish Nobel Prize Winners." *JINFO.org.*

[105] "Jewish Biographies: Nobel Prize Laureates." *Jewish Virtual Library.* http://www.jewishvirtuallibrary.org/jsource/Judaism/nobels.html

[106] "Douglas D. Osheroff - Biographical." *Nobelprize.org.* Nobel Media AB 2014. Web. 7 Nov 2016. <http://www.nobelprize.org/nobel_prizes/physics/laureates/1996/osheroff-bio.html>

[107] "Israel's Religiously Divided Society: Comparisons Between Jews in Israel and the U.S." *Pew Research Center,* 8 March 2016. http://www.pewforum.org/2016/03/08/comparisons-between-jews-in-israel-and-the-u-s/

[108] "Israel's Religiously Divided Society: Identity." *Pew Research Center,* 8 March 2016. http://www.pewforum.org/2016/03/08/comparisons-between-jews-in-israel-and-the-u-s/

[109] Ibid.

[110] Ibid.

[111] Katz Miller, Susan. "The Case for Raising Your Child with Two Religions." *Time,* 6 November 2013. http://ideas.time.com/2013/11/06/the-case-for-raising-your-child-with-two-religions/

[112] "One-in-Five U.S. Adults Were Raised in Interfaith Homes." *Pew Research Center,* 26 October 2016. http://www.pewforum.org/2016/10/26/one-in-five-u-s-adults-were-raised-in-interfaith-homes/

[113] Ibid.

[114] Allen, Susie. "Religious Upbringing Associated with Less Altruism, Study Finds." *UChicagoNews, The University of Chicago*, 5 November 2015. https://news.uchicago.edu/article/2015/11/05/religious-upbringing-associated-less-altruism-study-finds

[115] Tobin, Andrew. "Jason Segel Opens Up to Marc Maron About Childhood As Jewish Outsider." *Haaretz*, 31 July 2015.

[116] Matthew 13: 1-9

[117] "A Portrait of Jewish Americans: Connection with and Attitudes Toward Israel." *Pew Research Center*, 1 October 2013. http://www.pewforum.org/2013/10/01/chapter-5-connection-with-and-attitudes-towards-israel/

[118] "A Portrait of Jewish Americans." *Pew Research Center*, 1 October 2013. http://www.pewforum.org/2013/10/01/jewish-american-beliefs-attitudes-culture-survey/

[119] Ibid.

[120] Ibid.

[121] Ibid.

[122] Ibid.

[123] "Holocaust Encyclopedia: Escape from German-Occupied Europe." *United States Holocaust Memorial Museum*, Washington, D.C., (last update: 2 July 2016.) https://www.ushmm.org/wlc/en/article.php?ModuleId=10005470

[124] "Immigration to Israel: British Restrictions on Jewish Immigration to Palestine (1919 - 1942)." *Jewish Virtual Library*. http://www.jewishvirtuallibrary.org/jsource/History/mandate.html

[125] Bender, Lee S. and Verlin, Jerome R. "We Never Left: The Jews' Continuous Presence in the Land of Israel." *The Algemeiner*, 11 September 2016. https://www.algemeiner.com/2016/09/11/we-never-left-the-jews-continuous-presence-in-the-land-of-israel/

[126] Sobel, Jerrold L. "No One Is Stealing Palestinian Land." *American Thinker*, 13 November 2011. http://www.americanthinker.com/articles/2011/11/no_one_is_stealing_palestin ian_land.html

[127] Dershowitz, Alan (2003). *The Case for Israel* (p. 19). Hoboken, New Jersey: John Wiley & Sons, Inc.

[128] Ibid.

[129] Williams, Dan. "Netanyahu Turns to Bible in Tussle over Jerusalem." *Reuters*, 12 May 2010. http://www.reuters.com/article/us-palestinians-israel-jerusalem-idUSTRE64B2EY20100512

[130] Name has been changed to protect the privacy of the individual mentioned.

---

[131] "A Portrait of Jewish Americans: Chapter 3: Jewish Identity." *Pew Research Center*, 1 October 2013. http://www.pewforum.org/2013/10/01/chapter-3-jewish-identity/

[132] Ibid.

[133] Lew, Yossi. "What Does Aliyah Mean?" *Chabad.org.* http://www.chabad.org/library/article_cdo/aid/1584066/jewish/What-Does-Aliyah-Mean.htm

[134] "Law of Return 5710-1950." *Israel Ministry of Foreign Affairs*, 5 July 1950. http://www.mfa.gov.il/mfa/mfa-archive/1950-1959/pages/law%20of%20return%205710-1950.aspx

[135] Omer-Man, Michael. "This Week in History: Jewish Right to Aliya Becomes Law." *The Jerusalem Post*, 8 July 2011. http://www.jpost.com/Features/In-Thespotlight/This-Week-in-History-Jewish-right-to-aliya-becomes-law

[136] Mischling is singular, while mischlinge is plural.

[137] Cohen, Kenneth. "What Is Erev Rav." *The Times of Israel*, 11 February 2016. http://blogs.timesofisrael.com/what-is-erev-rav/

[138] The Sin of the Golden Calf is described in Exodus 32-34.

[139] Ibid.

[140] Aderet, Ofer. "Jews Are Not Descended from Khazars, Hebrew University Historian Says." *Haaretz*, 26 June 2014. http://www.haaretz.com/jewish/features/1.601287

[141] Yanover, Yori. "Study Finds No Evidence of Khazar Origin for Ashkenazi Jews." *The Jewish Press*, 23 February 2014. http://www.jewishpress.com/news/breaking-news/study-finds-no-evidence-of-khazar-origin-for-ashkenazi-jews/2014/02/23/

[142] Price, Roger. "Ginger Jews." *The Jewish Journal*, 16 June 2015. http://www.jewishjournal.com/judaismandscience/item/ginger_jews

[143] Philologos. "Redheaded Warrior Jews." *The Forward*, 12 August 2009. http://forward.com/culture/111973/redheaded-warrior-jews/

[144] Price, Roger. "Ginger Jews." *The Jewish Journal*, 16 June 2015. http://www.jewishjournal.com/judaismandscience/item/ginger_jews

[145] Shields, Jacqueline. "Modern Jewish History: The Tribes Today - Kohens, Levis & Yisraels." *Jewish Virtual Library.* http://www.jewishvirtuallibrary.org/jsource/Judaism/tribes1.html

[146] Jacobs, Rabbi Louis. "Levites Today." *My Jewish Learning.* http://www.myjewishlearning.com/article/levites/

[147] "Who Are Kohanim, or Jewish 'Priests'?" *My Jewish Learning.* http://www.myjewishlearning.com/article/kohanim-jewish-priests/

[148] Kleiman, Rabbi Yaakov. "The Cohanim - DNA Connection." *Aish*, 12 January 2000. http://www.aish.com/ci/sam/48936742.html

[149] "Jewish Gen-ealogy by Genetics." *JewishGen.* http://www.jewishgen.org/DNA/genbygen.html

[150] Name has been changed to protect the anonymity of all my living relatives. The actual surname was similar, and the name here is used merely as an example in order to get across the right idea.

[151] Both my grandparents' names have been changed.

[152] O'Neill, Claire. "What Did a '40s Census-Taker Look Like?", "From the Library of 'Life.' " *NPR,* 5 April 2012. http://www.npr.org/sections/pictureshow/2012/04/04/149988708/what-did-a-40s-census-taker-look-like

[153] Muraskin, Bennett. "Jewish Surnames Explained." *Slate,* 8 January 2014. http://www.slate.com/blogs/lexicon_valley/2014/01/08/ashkenazi_names_the_etymology_of_the_most_common_jewish_surnames.html

[154] Muraskin, Bennett. "Follow-Up: Jewish Surnames Explained." *Slate,* 30 January 2014. http://www.slate.com/blogs/lexicon_valley/2014/01/30/jewish_names_the_etymology_and_meaning_of_ashkenazi_jewish_surnames.html

[155] Spiro, Rabbi Ken. "History Crash Course #44: The Jews of Spain." *Aish,* 8 September 2001. http://www.aish.com/jl/h/cc/48950501.html

[156] Beider, Alexander. "Names and Naming." *YIVO Encyclopedia of Jews in Eastern Europe,* 7 September 2010. 23 November 2016 <http://www.yivoencyclopedia.org/article.aspx/Names_and_Naming>.

[157] Muraskin, Bennett. "Jewish Surnames Explained." *Slate,* 8 January 2014. http://www.slate.com/blogs/lexicon_valley/2014/01/08/ashkenazi_names_the_etymology_of_the_most_common_jewish_surnames.html

[158] Beider, Alexander. "Names and Naming." *YIVO Encyclopedia of Jews in Eastern Europe,* 7 September 2010. 23 November 2016

[159] Muraskin, Bennett. "Jewish Surnames Explained." *Slate,* 8 January 2014. http://www.slate.com/blogs/lexicon_valley/2014/01/08/ashkenazi_names_the_etymology_of_the_most_common_jewish_surnames.html

[160] The Statue of Liberty - Ellis Island Foundation, Inc. http://libertyellisfoundation.org/

[161] Rich, Tracey R. "Jewish Genealogy." *Judaism 101.* http://www.jewfaq.org/genealogy.htm

[162] Ibid.

[163] Name has been changed to protect the anonymity of my living relatives.

[164] Klier, John. "Pale of Settlement." *YIVO Encyclopedia of Jews in Eastern Europe,* 14 September 2010. 26 November 2016. <http://www.yivoencyclopedia.org/article.aspx/Pale_of_Settlement>.

[165] "Modern Jewish History: The Pale of Settlement." *Jewish Virtual Library.* http://www.jewishvirtuallibrary.org/jsource/History/pale.html

[166] Spiro, Rabbi Ken. "History Crash Course #56: Pale of Settlement." *Aish*, 15 December 2001. http://www.aish.com/jl/h/cc/48956361.html

[167] Green, David B. "This Day in Jewish History Catherine the Great Tells Jews Where They Can Live." *Haaretz*, 23 December 2013. http://www.haaretz.com/jewish/features/.premium-1.564905

[168] The Book of Esther, The Tanakh (The Bible)

[169] Genesis 17:15.

[170] Genesis 17:5.

[171] Alternate spelling: Chmielnicki

[172] Goldfoot, Nadene. "Ukraine's Massacre of Jews - Worse Than Nazis." *Jewish Facts from Portland*, 14 May 2013. http://jewishfactsfromportland.blogspot.com/2013/05/ukraines-massacre-of-jews-worse-than.html

[173] "Bogdan (Khmelnitski) Chmielnicki." *Jewish Virtual Library*. https://www.jewishvirtuallibrary.org/jsource/judaica/ejud_0002_0004_0_04259.html

[174] Spector, Shmuel and Wigoder, Geoffrey (2001). *The Encyclopedia of Jewish Life Before and During the Holocaust: A-J* (p133). NYU Press.

[175] Leiman, Shnayer Z. "From the Pages of Tradition: R. Raphael of Bershad's Commitment to Truth." *Leiman Library. Tradition 40:1*, 2007. Rabbinical Council of America. http://leimanlibrary.com/texts_of_publications/99.%20R.%20Raphael%20of%20Bershads%20Commitment%20to%20Truth.pdf

[176] Spector, Shmuel and Wigoder, Geoffrey (2001). *The Encyclopedia of Jewish Life Before and During the Holocaust: A-J* (p133). NYU Press.

[177] Ibid.

[178] "Encyclopedia Judaica: Bershad, Ukraine." *Jewish Virtual Library*. http://www.jewishvirtuallibrary.org/jsource/judaica/ejud_0002_0003_0_02804.html

[179] Veidlinger, Jeffrey (2013). *In the Shadow of the Shtetl: Small-Town Jewish Life in Soviet Ukraine* (p 19). Indiana University Press.

[180] "Encyclopedia Judaica: Bershad, Ukraine." *Jewish Virtual Library*. http://www.jewishvirtuallibrary.org/jsource/judaica/ejud_0002_0003_0_02804.html

[181] Bennett, G.H. (2012). The Nazi, The Painter and The Forgotten Story of the SS Road (p 113). London: Reaktion Books Ltd.

[182] Spector, Shmuel and Wigoder, Geoffrey (2001). *The Encyclopedia of Jewish Life Before and During the Holocaust: A-J* (p133). NYU Press.

[183] Bennett, G.H. (2012). The Nazi, The Painter and The Forgotten Story of the SS Road (p 113). London: Reaktion Books Ltd.

[184] Steeble, Susan K. "Two Tzaddiks: Part 4. The Bershad Synagogue." *Two Tzaddiks.* http://twotzaddiks.org/part4.html

[185] Levin, Sala. "The Biggest Genetic Jewish Myths of All Time." *Moment Magazine,* July-August 2012. http://www.momentmag.com/the-biggest-jewish-genetic-myths-of-all-time/

[186] Khan, Razib. "Which Grandparent Are You Most Related to?" *Slate,* 18 October 2013. http://www.slate.com/articles/health_and_science/human_genome/2013/10/a nalyze_your_child_s_dna_which_grandparents_are_most_genetically_related.ht ml

[187] Swayne, Anna. "Understanding Patterns of Inheritance: Where Did My DNA Come from? (And Why It Matters.)" *Ancestry,* 5 March 2014. http://blogs.ancestry.com/ancestry/2014/03/05/understanding-patterns-of-inheirtance-where-did-my-dna-come-from-and-why-it-matters/

[188] Starr, Dr. Barry. "Relatedness." *Stanford at the Tech: Understanding Genetics, The Tech, Museum of Innovation,* 5 September 2013. http://genetics.thetech.org/ask-a-geneticist/why-siblings-share-around-fifty-percent-their-dna

[189] Name has been changed to protect the identity of all living relatives.

[190] Name has been changed to protect the identity of all living relatives.

[191] Name has been changed.

[192] "Jewish Concepts: The Seven Noachide Laws." *Jewish Virtual Library.* http://www.jewishvirtuallibrary.org/jsource/Judaism/The_Seven_Noahide_Laws. html

[193] "Universal Morality: The Seven Noahide Laws." *Chabad.* http://www.chabad.org/therebbe/article_cdo/aid/62221/jewish/Universal-Morality.htm